In the making

Digital fabrication and disability

Ursula Kate Hurley
University of Salford

Series in Sociology

VERNON PRESS

www.vernonpress.com

In the Americas:
Vernon Press
1000 N West Street,
Suite 1200, Wilmington,
Delaware 19801
United States

In the rest of the world:
Vernon Press
C/Sancti Espiritu 17,
Malaga, 29006
Spain

Series in Sociology

Library of Congress Control Number: 2019951797

ISBN: 978-1-62273-928-8

Also available:

978-1-62273-330-9 [Hardback]; 978-1-62273-878-6 [PDF, E-Book]

Cover design by Vernon Press using elements made by Freepik from www.flaticon.com

bring us new tools then
register us designers

Scott Thurston, “for Roger Fowler”, PhD thesis

Table of contents

List of abbreviations

ADHD	Attention Deficit Hyperactivity Disorder
AHRC	Arts and Humanities Research Council
BBC	British Broadcasting Corporation
BSL	British Sign Language
BTEC	Business and Technology Education Council
CAD	Computer Aided Design
CBA	Center for Bits and Atoms
CIC	Community Interest Company
CNC	Computer Numerical Control
DOI	Digital Object Identifier
DRUK	Disability Rights UK
FabLab	Digital Fabrication Laboratory
GCSE	General Certificate of Secondary Education
HND	Higher National Diploma
JPEG	Joint Photographic Experts Group
LCD	Liquid Crystal Display
NESTA	National Endowment for Science, Technology and the Arts
PLA	Polylactic Acid
STEAM	Science Technology Engineering Arts and Math

List of figures and tables

Acknowledgements

Thanks to the Arts and Humanities Research Council, and project co-investigators Philip Connolly, founder of the Disability Resilience Network and formerly of Disability Rights UK and Nick Taylor at the University of Dundee. Thanks to our incredible supporters, too many to name individually but notably J Ahmed, Margaret Tullett, Eddie Kirkby, David Armson, The Manufacturing Institute, FabLabs Manchester, Ultimaker GB Ltd., Shaw Trust, and everyone else who gave so freely of their time and expertise. Special thanks to Jess Symons for her support and generosity in sharing facilitation techniques. Also huge thanks to Joe MacLeod-Iredale, director of Daedalus Design, for permission to post his MA thesis on the book's website, so that others can benefit from his groundbreaking research. Joe particularly wants to thank Fiona Velez Colby and Anne Fernie for their support with his MA research. We are also grateful to all at Challenge Multimedia for their careful evaluation of the project, and permission to share their report in this book (see Appendix 1). Thanks to Salford City Council, the BBC at MediaCityUK, Start in Salford, Princes Park Garden Centre and the Angel Centre, Salford for hosting our community workshops. Finally, grateful thanks to our project participants, without whom we would have achieved nothing.

A note to the reader

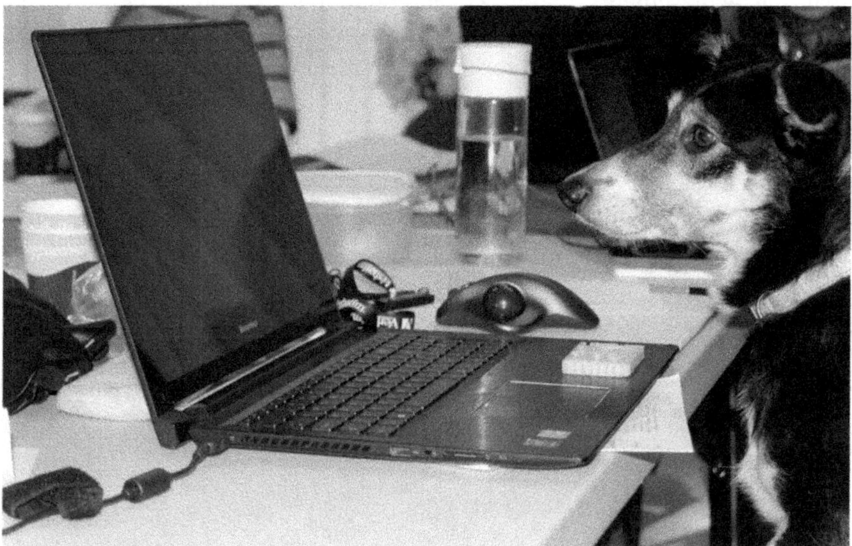

Figure 1.1. An assistance dog checks out her human companion's design.

Hello. Thanks for your interest in this book. I do hope that you will choose to go on and read it. To help inform your choice, I'd like to offer some indication of who I had in mind when I was writing. The book draws on the findings from a UK Research Council funded project, which set out to explore how disabled people might benefit from digital fabrication technologies, particularly 3D printing. As the book has its roots in a research project, there will be some citations and critical evaluation to help contextualize and evaluate the findings. However, this text is not just for academics! I have tried to write for anyone who has an interest in experiences of disability as they intersect with digital technologies, maker spaces, and/or creative processes. Alongside an account of the research, you can engage directly with the creations and experiences of our project participants. Our investigation was co-constructed with a network of disabled people from Greater Manchester, UK. To honor their contribution to the project, I have foregrounded their voices, images and experiences whenever possible – especially in Chapters 3 and 4. This book is not a technical or scientific guide to 3D printing. Rather, it employs approaches from the humanities in order to explore culturally and aesthetically the process of turning data into things. Some academic theories and concepts are employed to help me do this. However, I have included 'take-aways' at the end of each chapter. So, if the citations ever become too dry for your taste, you can find a user-friendly summary of insights and suggestions in bullet-point form. Whatever your reasons for reading, I hope that the achievements of our collaborators inspire you to consider the potential of digital fabrication in your own context, whether you are an expert maker or someone who is just curious about the possibilities.

Chapter 1

Introduction

Origins

The material in this book was generated by a UK Research Council funded project, "In the Making", which set out to explore how disabled people might benefit from digital fabrication technologies, and 3D printing in particular. The project began with the researchers visiting digital fabrication laboratories (often known as FabLabs or makerspaces) across the UK to learn about existing practices. We – researchers, collaborators and stakeholders – wanted to find out whether disabled people were already accessing makerspaces and, if so, what challenges they faced. Based on our findings (detailed in Chapter 2), we then organized a series of workshops to explore digital fabrication with disabled people. The research grant allowed us to buy entry-level 3D printing equipment, and expert creative and technical facilitation.

Over an 18-month period spanning 2015-16, we provided 3D printing equipment and approximately 100 hours of tuition to over 100 disabled people, their supporters, families and friends. Our mobile digital fabrication laboratory toured venues in Greater Manchester, a conurbation in the northwest of the UK which includes many communities affected by post-industrial decline. Our venues set out to be non-typical of the usual makerspace, which can imply that only the technically adept are welcome, in order to be accessible to as wide a range of people as possible. Sites included a garden center, the BBC at MediaCityUK, community arts centers and public libraries. In each location we invited people to play with the technology, ask questions, join ideas workshops and participate in training sessions.

The approach throughout was "I can make it". We used this phrase with conscious reference to the layers of meaning it contains. Alongside the sense of physically making a useful or beautiful object is the abstract sense of "making it" by succeeding in life, crossing the finish line, achieving a goal. We set out to show that digital fabrication can support the "I can make it" ethos through its ability to empower people who are traditionally excluded from economic success and social status (Connolly 2017). With Joe McLeod-Iredale, founder and director of Daedalus Design (http://www.daedalusdesign.org/), we developed an inclusive pedagogy entitled "Digital Fabrication for the 99%" (2016). You can read more about this on the book's website. Everyone, no matter their physical or mental capacities, was supported to be actively involved in the making process, be that expressing preferences via an interpreter, making a sketch, taking a photograph, or learning the software to an advanced level of independent practice. The outputs from these making sessions ranged from the practical (a dog tag), the assistive (a finger splint), the political (wearable text), to the aesthetic (abstract sculpture). People returned to work with us on multiple occasions and eventually demand outstripped the project's resources. Our Steering Group formulated a responsible exit strategy, which included signposting people to permanent makerspace provision, introducing them to key contacts, and facilitating their transition to longer-term, sustainable making activities.

The project concluded in 2016 with an exhibition and a conference bringing together interested parties to share learning and ways forward. Since then, we have been evaluating the research findings, writing up our conclusions, and considering how to take the project forward. The work of this book is to document the processes and products of our inclusive, mobile digital fabrication lab. Much more detail about what we did, what worked and what didn't will be offered in subsequent chapters. The remainder of the Introduction sets out some important points about technology, context, aims and objectives, research methods, language and ethics. If you're keen to see what people made during the workshops, you might want to skip straight to Chapter 3.

A note on the technology

What would you make, if you could make anything you could imagine? This is the question facing anyone who engages with the FabLab environment. That very act of imagining, of selecting and committing to an envisaged but not yet physically present product, offers insights into needs and desires. What is the story of that design? How did it come to be? The basic principles of digital fabrication – the transformation from concept to physical entity – offer intriguing possibilities for aesthetic and cultural readings. Digital fabrication is epitomized by Neil Gershenfeld's now iconic phrase: "the ability to turn data into things and things into data" (2012, 44). If you're already familiar with digital fabrication technologies, then feel free to skip this section. For the rest of us, digital fabrication is summarized as follows:

- A person wanting to digitally fabricate an object begins with an idea for a design. They, or someone skilled in CAD (computer-aided design), will "build" a digital version of the object on a computer and save it as a design file. The type of file will vary depending upon the design software being used. There is a lot of free open source design software available, as well as costly professional programs.

- The design file is then exported to a digitally-controlled machine, typically a laser cutter, CNC router or 3D printer, which translates the computer code into physical movements.
- Heating, cutting or shaping actions are applied to solid material which is formed into the realized version of the computer design file.
- Through computer-controlled manipulation of a physical substance, the design file materializes into a tangible object. With our project's 3D printers, you loaded spools of plastic filament instead of the paper and ink that you load into conventional 2D inkjet or laser printers.
- Or, vice-versa, a physical object can be scanned and encoded as digital information. The process works in both directions.
- Whatever the manner of the file's creation, this digital version of the object means that, in theory, infinite physical versions of it may be produced.
- With some knowledge of computer programs, it is also possible to modify or adapt the file using open-source software.
- Any of these digital versions may be posted online for others to download, replicate or modify further.

Many devices can be employed in digital fabrication, and it is not the work of this text to provide a detailed account of their technical attributes. Throughout, as above, I will offer basic summaries of the principles involved, assuming no expert knowledge on the part of the reader.

Our funding allowed us to secure the equipment necessary to produce simple 3D prints, together with expert facilitation from our local FabLab (http://www.traffordfablab.co.uk). Our project chose to work with 3D printers because they "make it remarkably clear how an idea (or at least the virtual, digitally designed representation of an idea) can become a material object" (Walter-Herrmann and Büching, 2013, 11). We used Ultimaker 2 printers for their accessible operation and appealing appearance (https://ultimaker.com/). These printers use software which "slices" the digital design into tiny topographical layers. The design is then realized physically by the incremental depositing of these layers via a print head which extrudes hot polylactic acid (PLA / plastic) filament, although more sophisticated printers can work with other materials and by different methods (e.g., solidifying powdered resin). Entry-level 3D printers are readily available to the home user and early adopters already share a wealth of designs via open source websites like Thingiverse (https://www.thingiverse.com/).

These collaborative, open-source qualities lead many commentators to identify digital fabrication as an emergent and disruptive technology which is reaching a critical mass in terms of worldwide users (Gershenfeld 2005; Landay 2009). Beyond individual engagement with this technology, a global community of makers is evolving, in which, "For the first time in history, laypeople can participate in the product design and manufacturing process by directly interacting with the underlying hardware and software" (Lau, Mitani and Igarashi 2012,76). The implications for the democratization and personalization of manufacturing raise profound questions about intellectual property and economic models leading some, such as technology commentator Chris Anderson, to hail the "maker" movement as the dawning of a new industrial revolution (Anderson 2012). Such claims indicate the radical potential of the technology and the communities growing around it. The starting point of our project was to investigate whether disabled people could participate in and benefit from this supposed revolution.

Hopefully, this brief summary makes clear that digital fabrication is potentially a game-changer for the way that industry manufactures and distributes the things that people design, while democratizing the role of the designer. We were interested in the technology's potential to "change the game" for disabled people, resituating them as designers, makers and discerning consumers of bespoke products, who are empowered to move beyond "one size fits no-one" mass-market economics.

What this summary fails to capture, however, is the sense of wonder, the feeling that we are witnessing science fiction become science fact as an object that existed as an idea, and then a computer file, materializes in front of us. Having witnessed on many occasions with many different people that moment of revelation, it is clear to me that there is a profound fascination in the transformation of digital information into a concrete thing, a compelling quality in the tactile emergence of an idea in the external reality of its maker. The sense of "magic", of revelation, seemed to be a near-universal experience in our participants (and our facilitators, who shared the privilege of playing midwife to someone's idea). The effect seemed to be intensified by the glitches and apparent capriciousness of this emergent technology, which is not yet entirely reliable. We witnessed this astonishment and deep compulsion again and again, in people of varied circumstances, backgrounds and abilities.

Such observations seem to resonate with Lucas D. Introna's description of wonder when an archaeologist encounters a newly-revealed artefact. He uses Graham Harman's concept of *allure* to explain "this bursting forth of the thing in its thingness" and likens the experience to "the image of a young child staring with wonder into an empty glass, or a pile of toys, as if everything that is important, wonderful and relevant is revealed there" (2014, 52). This staring with wonder is exactly what we saw again and again in the making space as a 3D print emerged. We felt instinctively that this allure was somehow to do with materiality, with the embodiment of the imagination. We also intuited that this quality of digital fabrication goes well beyond the ability to make useful stuff. There is something about being able to express thoughts and ideas in solid objects, unique to the maker's imagination, that causes this technology to be especially potent. The ability of 3D printers to evoke states of wonder is explored further in the political and creative strands of the project detailed below.

Re-framing the debate

Philip Connolly, founder of the Disability Resilience Network, is inspired by the "first mover" opportunity presented by emerging digital fabrication technology. He believes passionately that if people with disabilities could participate early in an emergent field, they could establish themselves as key players – creating the parameters of economic development rather than being obstructed by them. Since 3D printing is based on the idea of designing and manufacturing goods based on immediate and customized need, its processes may suit people who are generally excluded from mainstream markets. Disabled people are "experts by experience"; their circumstances are usually unique, each with a particular set of challenges. Motivated to explore these possibilities, in 2015, Philip contacted me, a creative writing academic at the University of Salford, and together we designed the research project that you are now reading about.

Disability Rights UK estimates that there are 3.6 million economically inactive disabled people in the UK, the majority of whom survive by claiming welfare benefits (http://www.disabilityrightsuk.org/). Global economic uncertainty and "austerity" Britain mean that disabled people have been particularly affected by changes to the UK welfare system. This, together with negative portrayals of benefits claimants in the mainstream media, intensifies the difficulties reported by the UK Government's official statistics, which found that disabled people are significantly more likely to live in poverty, to be unemployed, to be victims of crime, and to be discriminated against in all aspects of their lives (Department for Work and Pensions, 2014). Financial, educational and social disconnections therefore disproportionately affect disabled people and need urgently to be addressed. At the same time, technological developments and the digital economy are changing the ways we work, socialize, and learn. Might these changes be a means of addressing the barriers experienced by disabled people?

Collaborative and accessible by nature, the FabLab movement has a track-record of inclusive practice. For example, FabLab Manchester hosts the "Fability" project, which supports disabled people in making things that are of practical help in their day-to-day lives (http://fability.tumblr.com/). These are important first steps in demonstrating the potential of the technology and the recasting of disabled people as "makers" of solutions rather than recipients of "help". Such interventions, while highly worthwhile, do not extend further than making things to address physical problems. We wanted to explore whether disabled people could use FabLab facilities to make things that others may want to buy, and/or which may be of aesthetic as well as practical value.

What might prevent disabled makers from doing this for themselves? After all, many UK FabLabs offer free or subsidized training and lab time to individuals or community groups. However, access to such facilities is limited, often needs to be booked in advance, requires the user to know about the facility, travel there and enter it. Disability Rights UK believes that travel is one of the greatest barriers to disabled people. There is little if any published information on the accessibility of UK FabLabs – it takes a great deal of searching and one is unlikely to make the effort to attend a lab if its accessibility cannot be established in advance of a visit. We heard many stories of wasted journeys and discouraging experiences from our project participants. As established FabLabs need to fund themselves in an uncertain economic climate, they can move premises and change staff frequently. In addition, there can often be charges for materials, too. Travel, access, money and resources could all pose barriers to disabled people using existing makerspace provision (more on this in Chapter 2). Although several research projects involving digital fabrication have been funded by Research Councils UK, they are focused on scientific and commercial investigations. None of them explores the potential of digital fabrication to benefit disabled people in the way that our project attempted.

Scope and parameters

The focus of our investigation was to explore whether digital fabrication could be of use to those with lived experience of disability, not just practically (i.e. making assistive aids) but also in creative, political and economic terms. By "political", we mean raising awareness of disabled people's potential by positively challenging stereotypes about what they can do. We set out to do this by:

1. Mapping current inclusive FabLab provision in the UK and
2. Addressing issues of exclusion by taking mobile fabrication equipment into unusual or risky settings.

We aimed to test the premise that access to and training in digital fabrication can catalyze cultural change by:

1) making personalized aids and devices that allow disabled people to overcome barriers to economic participation in society,
2) making products that have a mass market and offer the prospect of jobs for other disabled and non-disabled people, and
3) exploring artistic and political making practices, co-creating resources in a period when the provision of state resources is reducing.

Our mobile fabrication laboratory offered opportunities to learn, receive training, form collaborative partnerships, and experiment in thinking, making and identity. Via inclusive practices and adaptations, the laboratory sought to avoid the digital divide whereby new technology can act to exclude people, e.g. touch screen technology excluding visually impaired people. By the end of the project, we aimed to have:

1) brought FabLab facilities to users in their own setting
2) offered bespoke training and facilitation, designed around the expressed needs of users
3) offered a safe "making space" in which disabled users became part of a supportive community of practice, in which all materials were provided free of charge
4) offered a bridge into more advanced practice at established FabLabs
5) explored the entrepreneurial potential of what people make, recasting disabled people as innovators
6) explored the political potential of "critical making" in terms of expressing wants, needs, and raising cultural visibility
7) explored 3D fabrication as a creative, "fabulous" process, in which practicalities may be disregarded in favor of the imagination, offering ways into self-understanding and enhanced self-esteem
8) to have done so by co-constructing the application and evaluation of inclusive, collaborative making practices, with the findings contributing to academic debate and policy impacts.

How far we achieved these aims will be evaluated at the conclusion of the book.

Managing risks and failures

We set out with some fine aims, expressed in language designed to convince our funders that their money would be well spent. In effect, the "In the Making" project loaded basic 3D printing equipment into the trunk of my car, and we drove it and some expert facilitators around the local area trying to engage disabled people with the technology. As far as we are aware, nothing like this had ever been attempted before in the UK. Careful ethics and risk assessment procedures were therefore of paramount importance and informed our practice throughout. I summarize the main concerns here. Detailed discussions unfold in the following chapters.

Where did we begin? We spoke to established organizations and networks, identifying gatekeepers who might invite us into their communities. By starting out with established and visible networks, we risked engaging only with people who are already involved with disabled identities, campaigns and activities, overlooking the profoundly excluded, who may be able to benefit most fully from access to digital fabrication practices. We also took care to avoid imposing categories and identities on diverse individuals. Participation in the inclusive FabLab sessions in no way depended upon fulfilling a particular definition of disability; anyone showing an interest was introduced to the equipment and made aware of the open access sessions offered at established FabLabs in Greater Manchester. Issues of access and the equitable distribution of limited resources were considered throughout the project's design and deployment, and they are unfolded in more detail in later chapters.

We followed the established wisdom of community-based researchers (see Chittenden 2014) by starting with existing networks and well-used community spaces to raise our project's profile in the local area before trying to bridge further into the harder to reach places. The project team all brought with them existing partnerships and contacts. We hoped these networks and collaborations would expand as the project progressed. Reaching from those networks into spaces of exclusion was a key challenge. For example, we brought our FabLab into a garden center run by and for people with intellectual disabilities. The risk here was that we imposed an identity and an activity upon people who were essentially a "captive audience". These challenges are explored further in subsequent chapters. We also took risks by offering the fabrication facilities in unexpected spaces, such as community centers, or the BBC at MediaCityUK.

Further risks included the theft of or damage to the equipment by trusting it to community use and ownership. In fact, the equipment was treated with great respect by each community we visited and survived intact to be placed on long term loan at Salford's Morson Makerspace for use by students and local people. However, some venues did express concerns about security and the implications for their insurance policies, and in some cases declined to host our equipment due to mainly unfounded anxieties.

From the outset, we designed the project to anticipate potential lack of demand/interest in the facilities (we had no idea who might engage), although this concern proved to be at the wrong end of the scale: the project was overwhelmed by the enthusiastic demand for its offer, and sometimes struggled to meet the needs of participants as time and resources became stretched. As discussed, the project team considered constantly the potential failure to reach the excluded and disconnected (how do we know who and where they are? Do they *want* to be included?). From the number and diversity of participants, including those with multiple and profound physical and mental challenges, the project team believes that we did as well as we could with the time and resources available to reach as many people as possible. Caring, travel and subsistence costs were paid wherever practicable but as word spread and people from geographically distant locations began coming to work with us, support budgets were used up. We could always do more to engage people, however, and a key element of our future work will be to scale up the resources available.

Another risk was what users might make. Gershenfeld (2012, 47) reassures us on this point: "Even if 3-D printers could be controlled, hurting people is already a well-met market demand. Cheap weapons can be found anywhere in the world. CBA'S experience running FabLabs in conflict zones has been that they are used as an alternative to fighting." In fact, none of our participants attempted to make anything that could have been physically dangerous. Some had heard the story of the 3D printed gun but considered it to be an overelaborate method of creating something that would do nothing to improve their lives and was, in fact, ineffective (there are far easier ways of acquiring functional, conventional weapons in the areas in which we worked).

The final and perhaps the most serious risk was that of our participants failing to create. We were mindful always of our responsibilities to the people who chose to engage with our project. As will be discussed in subsequent chapters, many of our participants came to us from marginalized positions, with low self-esteem, battered by life-long struggles with painful and debilitating conditions, as well as dealing with health and social care systems which often positioned them as passive recipients. We had to take great care to empower our participants as creators, and to manage any technical glitches as part of a creative process, framing the experience as a positive narrative rather than confirming negative perceptions about their own ability. As reflective practitioners, the project team sought to frame any of these (or other) potential risks or failures as learning opportunities, the results of which are included in the following chapters.

Methodology

"In the Making" staged a co-constructed inquiry in which researchers and participants worked together as equals to develop inclusive making sessions that explored the issues outlined above. We had scant examples to guide us. As Matt Ratto notes, "using shared practices of making to enhance [...] research has been infrequently applied and little studied" (2011, 254). We aimed to address this gap in existing research. Illustrated in Table 1.1, we used Ratto's approach to structure our activities, practically and conceptually facilitating environments in which inclusive, collaborative making practices could develop.

Table 1.1. Timetable of project activities.

Stage One. Months 1-6. "Review of relevant literature and compilation of useful concepts and theories. This is mined for specific ideas that can be explored through fabrication" (Ratto 2011, 253). We proposed to adapt Ratto's three-stage critical making project to structure our investigation.		
Investigators to visit 12 established UK FabLabs to ascertain whether presumed low usage by disabled people is 1. In fact, low, 2. Linked to poor accessibility, 3. Due to a lack of appropriate marketing, or 4. The absence of demand. Output: foundational insights from which to design our inclusive FabLab.	Investigators to work with FabLabs UK (www.fablabsuk.co.uk) and the FabLab Foundation (www.fabfoundation.org) to explore engagement with disabled users. Output: best practices and barriers identified.	Investigators and collaborators form project steering group, chaired by Connolly, with members invited initially from Salford Disability Forum, and the Broughton Trust. Output: co-constructed governance mechanism which feeds back to senior management at Disability Rights UK.
Stage Two. Months 7-12. "Scholars and stakeholders jointly extend knowledge and skills in relevant technical areas to provide the means for conceptual exploration" (Ibid.).		
Responsive management	Continuous Evaluation	Mobile FabLab provision
Workshop with Steering Group, stakeholders and potential users to plan the nature, timing and format of FabLab provision. Followed by regular meetings and input from DRUK. Are we being inclusive? Are we connecting effectively with appropriate audiences? Output: co-construction, partnership working.	Working together, with input from arthur+martha to decide how and when activities will be evaluated. Embedding reflective practice into activities, capturing insights. Output: generation of documentary material; capturing needs and wishes of users; adapting delivery to accommodate them.	86 hours of facilitation by FabLab Manchester and arthur+martha were budgeted. Their use will be determined by the Steering Group and participants. Output: training and provision of opportunities in places where this technology is not usually present.

Stage Three. Months 13-18. "Exploring various configurations and alternative possibilities, and using them to express, critique, and extend relevant concepts, theories, and models" (Ibid.).		
Evaluation	Dissemination	Application
A reflective workshop was held to co-construct findings, insights and recommendations. Legacy, sustainability and exit strategy also considered. The investigators met to share experiences. Where the synergies, where the gaps?	Co-curated exhibition including products of fabrication and documents of process. Free symposium to present findings at MediaCityUK, to which key policy-makers and business representatives were invited, along with participants. Conference presentations and publications by investigators.	Academic: to initiate a conversation between the arts, disability studies and human-computer interaction, with a focus on pathways to social benefits. Practical: What might be scaled up? Which agencies involved? Initial planning for larger bid.
Note: the three distinct research strands (entrepreneurial, political and creative making) interweave throughout the above, each championed by a research lead. A key element of the academic evaluation, dissemination and application was to consider the relative usefulness of each approach, and the productiveness of their combination in this and future activities.		

The project is titled "In the Making" because we see different conceptions and processes of making as being key to the research and practical aspects of the project activities. The emergent concept of "critical making", as used in Design Studies, infused the ethos and approach of the project. Critical making is based upon participatory, collaborative activities, in which the collective processes of production become tools for co-constructing research, its interpretation and significance. Research framed in this way has notions of community and connection at its core. DiSalvo points out that this approach goes beyond asking people what kinds of products they would find useful. Instead, critical making involves "potential users and stakeholders as collaborators in the design process, as themselves designers" (DiSalvo 2011, 97). Our methodology went further still. We intended our collaborators to progress beyond designing to become makers; to employ the concept of "critical making" in the hope of bringing about a paradigm shift, so that those involved in FabLab activities are not just "co-designers" but "co-manufacturers". In short, to investigate whether FabLabs could have a role in recasting disabled people as digital entrepreneurs who overcome barriers through their own creativity.

In so doing, we aimed to "question and transform how and who can make credible and actionable knowledge" (Wylie et al. 2014, 116). Could a 3D print designed and made by a disabled person become "actionable knowledge" in terms of the insights it might offer? Such a methodology serves our collaborative, interdisciplinary investigation well. Ratto explains how a shared making process brings everyone together into a "collective frame" (2011, 253). At the same time as bringing people together, our critical making approach helped us to negotiate our working relationships: "allowing disciplinary and epistemic differences to be both highlighted and hopefully overcome" (Ratto 2011, 253). As detailed in subsequent chapters, disciplinary differences posed challenges – how does a computer scientist talk to a creative writer? – as did the epistemic differences arising from how we "know" things in differently-embodied perspectives. For example, what I "know" from my embodied situation may be radically divergent from what someone on the autistic spectrum "knows".

To manage these complex dynamics, we sub-divided our investigations into the three distinct but interconnected strands detailed above, which both maximized the effectiveness of the expertise available and mapped on to the "hybrid practice" of critical making proposed by Ratto: "a mode of materially productive engagement that is intended to bridge the gap between creative physical and conceptual exploration" (2011, 252). There is little more apt than a 3D printer to literally make a bridge from theory to practice. 3D printers engage people, they make material things, they invite creative responses, and they also deal in abstract, virtual designs. In fact, a 3D printer *is* a bridge between an idea and its manifestation. In co-constructing this hybrid creative/physical/conceptual exploration of 3D printing, we intended to explore whether our research, far from being esoteric, could light the path to practices that improve people's lives in tangible ways. Perhaps one day, government policy will be to offer every disabled person a training course in digital fabrication technology and a business startup grant, rather than consigning them to a life of passive welfare payments.

Underpinning research

The research represented here arises from a UK Arts and Humanities Research Council "Connected Communities" innovation project run jointly by Disability Rights UK, the University of Salford and the University of Dundee: "In the Making: a co-constructed mapping and feasibility study of digital fabrication labs and their potential to catalyze cultural change" (AH/M006026/1). This original monograph draws on that project and represents the product of multiple collaborative endeavor. The conclusions set out here draw on a developmental trajectory spanning several years and could not have been achieved without the contribution of our participants and collaborators, fellow researchers, first readers, editors and peer reviewers. Key building blocks in the articulation of the project's achievements include the following conference proceedings and reports:

- Nick Taylor, Ursula Hurley, and Philip Connolly (2016) "Making community: the wider role of makerspaces in public life", in:

Proceedings of CHI 2016 (Human-Computer Interaction conference) SIGCHI (Special Interest Group on Human Computer Interaction). DOI:10.1145/2858036.2858073

- Nick Taylor, Philip Connolly, Ursula Hurley, and Joe Macleod-Iredale (2016), "Breadth, depth and height: early findings on engaging disabled people with digital fabrication "in*: CHI 2016 Workshop: Fabrication & HCI: Hobbyist Making, Industrial Production, and Beyond*, 08/05/2016, Salzburg. https://hci.sbg.ac.at/wp-content/uploads/2015/11/Breadth_Depth_Height.pdf
- Nick Taylor and Ursula Hurley (2016) *Empowering disabled people with digital fabrication : insights from the "In the Making" Project - submission to All Party Parliamentary Group on Disability* [cited as an example of good practice in the final report: The All Party Parliamentary Group (APPG) on Disability, "Ahead of the Arc" – a Contribution to Halving the Disability Employment Gap, 2016, 52-53] https://www.disabilityrightsuk.org/sites/default/files/pdf/AheadoftheArc9Dec2016.pdf]

Although the above publications are not referenced directly in this book, I remain indebted to my co-authors for the contextual value of this work in developing my thinking.

Additionally, three published articles are reworked in some of the substance of this book. They are:

- Ursula Hurley (2018) "The Embodiment of Pure Thought"? Digital Fabrication, Disability, and New Possibilities for Auto/Biography, *a/b: Auto/Biography Studies*, 33:2, 285-300, DOI: 10.1080/08989575.2018.1445509
- Jessica Symons & Ursula Hurley (2018) Strategies for connecting low income communities to the creative economy through play: two case studies in Northern England, *Creative Industries Journal*, DOI: 10.1080/17510694.2018.1453770
- Ursula Hurley (2019) Printing a New Story: Self-representation, Disability, and Digital Fabrication, *European Journal of Life Writing*, DOI: 10.21827/ejlw.8.35555

I am hugely grateful to Sarah Brophy and Ricia Chansky for their enlightening editorial comments on "The Embodiment of Pure Thought", and to my co-author Jessica Symons for adding her anthropological insights, as well as the peer reviewers and journal editor Graeme Harper for their contribution to the *Creative Industries* article. Similarly, Clare Brant, Rob Gallagher and the peer reviewers involved in the *European Journal of Life Writing* article helped to push my thinking along. All three pieces are published open access under a Creative Commons 4.0 license and are freely available via the DOIs above.

Finally, my blogpost, "Little Fictions, Big Questions" for the Thresholds short story resource underpins my thinking about miniaturization in Chapter 3: http://thresholds.chi.ac.uk/little-fictions-big-questions/

A note on language, ethics and approaches

When I refer to "we" and "our" project, I mean to include everyone who contributed to the project. Broadly, the research leads comprised: the author, a novice 3D printer with a background in creative writing, in collaboration with Philip Connolly, founder of the Disability Resilience Network, and Nick Taylor, a human-computer interaction specialist at the University of Dundee. Technical advice and facilitation came from FabLabs Manchester, pedagogical input from Joe MacLeod-Iredale of Daedalus Design, and creative facilitation from local community artists, particularly arthur+martha CIC. A local steering group, drawn from participants, researchers and stakeholders, met regularly to guide the project's progress, and to resolve issues of access and ethics. The project has ethical approval from The University of Salford, and each participant co-constructed a personalized permissions document, detailing, according to their expressed preferences, how much of their data the researchers could use and in what ways. All the project materials appearing in this book were generated by people who have given permission for their work to be used in academic publications. However, names have been changed due to the personal nature of the material. Reference to "we" and "our" implies the collective membership of the project – researchers, facilitators and collaborators.

"Communities should not fear or ignore digital fabrication. Better ways to build things can help build better communities" (Gershenfeld 2012, 50). From the outset, we reminded ourselves regularly that "disabled" and "community" are problematic and contested terms. When we talk about disabled people, we use the term to mean "anyone with lived experience of disability or health issues", as articulated by Disability Rights UK (https://www.disabilityrightsuk.org/). For a critical account of how such terminology may contribute to the reclaiming of the term "disabled" (in the same way that the word "queer" is being reclaimed), please see Alice Wexler and John Derby's 2015 article, "Art in Institutions: The Emergence of (Disabled) Outsiders" in *Studies in Art Education: A Journal of Issues and Research.* We acknowledge that "disability" and "disabled" are shifting categories, and ones which most of us will inhabit at some point in our lives, if not constantly.

In setting out these issues, it is also important to state that our inclusive digital fabrication laboratory was not prescriptive in specifying what was to be made, by whom or how. It was not a "ghetto of provision" in which only people meeting a particular definition of "disabled" could participate. We encouraged collaborative partnerships with non-disabled people and the making of products for mainstream markets. We positioned collaborative making involving disabled and non-disabled people as a key mechanism for addressing exclusion and disconnection. However, we acknowledge conceptual and practical difficulties in how we define and apply ideas about community and disability. While it is evident that disabled people do experience social isolation and economic exclusion because of their circumstances, it would be overly simplistic to assume that all disabled people are part of or would want to identify as being members of a "community of disability". How we connected with potential co-constructors and collaborators is a question with no easy answers and is an issue that we grappled with throughout the project.

The term FabLab/makerspace frequently occurs in the literature surrounding digital fabrication practices. Neil Gershenfeld established a standard inventory of digital fabrication equipment for makerspaces, or FabLabs, at the Massachusetts Institute for Technology's Center for Bits and Atoms (CBA). The FabLab movement is now a global network, and makerspaces which are members of the network must adhere to a common set of standards and practices: http://fab.cba.mit.edu/about/charter/

Now that's all cleared up, we're ready to move into the detail of what we learned from the project. But first, here's a summary of take-aways from Chapter 1.

Take-aways

- Our project took 3D printers and expert facilitators into community venues in northwest England. We worked with disabled people to understand how digital fabrication technologies might benefit them. We think that this is the first time anything like this has been attempted in the UK.
- Digital fabrication is potentially a game-changer for the ways in which industry manufactures and distributes the products that people want. We were interested in its potential to "change the game" for disabled people – could they become

digital entrepreneurs who overcome barriers through their own creativity?

- Despite the transformative potential of this technology, little research has been done on how disabled people might engage with it. FabLab culture is open and inclusive, but the precarity of makerspace provision means that there are challenges to access the facilities.
- Our project considered risks and failures very carefully, doing everything possible to ensure that participants had a positive, creative experience despite the limitations on resource. People engaged enthusiastically, respected the equipment, and had little interest in making anything dangerous or illegal.
- We used the concept of "critical making" to inform our collaborative approach to the project, and we structured our activities around three research themes: entrepreneurial, political and creative.
- Our project took great care with language and ethics, using "we" and "us" to denote the collaborative nature of the research, and mindfully reclaiming the word "disabled" as a fluid category which includes anyone who chooses to identify as such.

Chapter 2

Makerspace Mapping

In the first phase of the "In the Making" project, the researchers surveyed makerspaces across the country to learn about existing practices and identify potential benefits and challenges for disabled makers. The three research leads, Connolly, Hurley and Taylor visited 12 established UK makerspaces, some official FabLabs, others less formally constituted, in as wide a variety of contexts and locations as possible. As Figure 2.1 illustrates, makerspaces are typically informal, diverse spaces in which social activities such as making tea are just as important as the technologies. Further discussion of the wellbeing benefits of makerspaces follows in subsequent chapters.

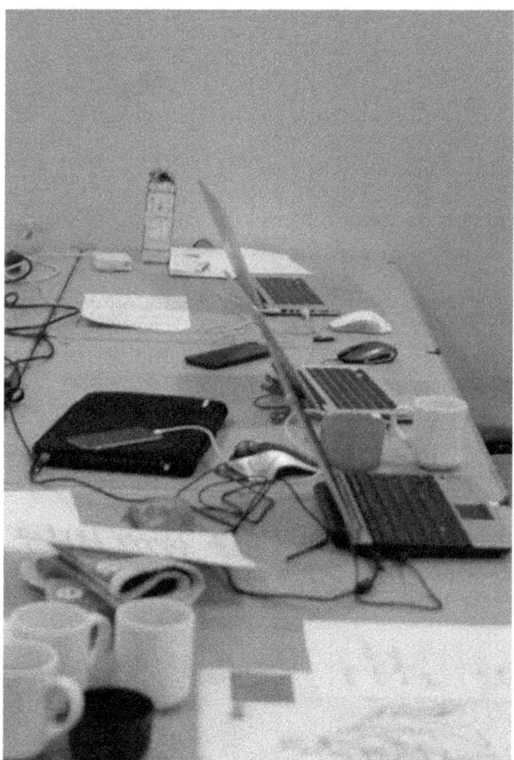

Figure 2.1. A tangle of wires and teacups epitomizes makerspace culture.

The objective of our site visits was to ascertain whether presumed low usage of makerspaces by disabled people is:

1. In fact, low
2. Linked to poor accessibility
3. Due to a lack of appropriate marketing
4. The absence of demand.

A standard interview protocol was used at each visit, to structure conversations and to ensure a level of consistency in the approach of different investigators in different times and places.

Interview protocol

Background

- Please, could you tell us about how the FabLab was set up?
- What were you aiming to do?
- What sort of people utilize the facilities at the moment?
- Has this changed over time?
- What are people's reasons for using the facilities? Discuss in reference to aims of the project:
    - economic prosperity/entrepreneurship
    - self-expression, self-representation
    - activism, raising awareness, disabled rights
- What support is available to people wanting to get involved?
- What is your business model? Future business plans? (No obligation to provide commercially sensitive information)

Existing Use by Disabled People

- Has there been any existing use of your facilities by disabled people, or any expressions of interest?
- Are there any success stories?
- If not, why do you think that is?

- Are you aware of it happening anywhere else?
- What difficulties do you think might be encountered in making that happen?
- Do you see ways of overcoming those problems?
- Is disabled access something that you've thought about in the past?
- How has it factored into your planning?

Outreach

- Do you do any work with charities or similar community organization, either in regard to disability or other causes?
- What other outreach activities take place?
Thank you very much for your time and expertise.

Protocol ends

The conversations were recorded (with permission) to be used in future analysis. Each investigator also produced a summary of their visit as soon as possible afterwards, to capture the key insights and distinctive qualities of each space we visited. I reproduce each of those summaries here, to give a flavor of the diversity of making practices and cultures in the UK.

Individual visit summaries

57 North, Aberdeen

31st March 2015

57 North is a hackerspace located on Union Street, which has been running since August 2013. In contrast to other spaces that have been visited so far, 57 North is a very lo-fi operation with a limited budget. They operate from a single small office, cluttered with equipment. The space has around 15 regular members paying £20 per month. These are mostly people from the university with an existing involvement in computer science or engineering. Potential members typically find them online or at a hacking event, but their reasons for joining weren't questioned—for them, it is a natural state of existence.

Where other spaces focus on digital manufacturing, 57 North is more focused on the development and customization of computer hardware and software. Members work on small individual projects, typically with the philosophy that individuals can do things better and cheaper than commercial providers and learn from the experience at the same time.

For members, the social aspect of the space is most important. Most of the members could afford to replicate the equipment and facilities, but it was important to have somewhere to go where they could talk to likeminded people and be socially engaged during otherwise solitary tasks. Peer learning is an important aspect of this and members are generally very willing to help each other. This is in contrast to more organized makerspaces, which are more about providing a service. Unlike other organizations, they don't have a leadership or exist as an arts organization: they just want the space.

They're quite politically active as a group, particularly in relation to digital rights, privacy etc. There is some interest in businesses from some members, and others are interested in engaging with artists. They do run events for members of the public, typically small workshops in larger events with simple electronics activities. The goal of these events is to make a little money and perhaps find new members, rather than loftier goals about educating. However, they have shown some interest in getting unemployed people into the space as a way of building skills and helping them find employment.

Accessibility is very poor. The space is a single office located on the third floor with no elevator. The space itself is very small and cramped. They are very aware of this problem and want the facilities to be available to everyone but can't currently afford to move. For at least one member who has recently undergone a leg amputation, this means being unable to attend.

ArtLink, Edinburgh

20th May 2015

ArtLink is an arts and disability organization that has been running in Edinburgh since 1984. They run a variety of art projects with participants with varying degrees of disability, although they tend towards those with profound learning difficulties. For these participants, the artwork is very much a form of communication and a tool to open up new ways of understanding and interacting with the world around them.

They describe their method as being quite unique: their projects tend to run in the very long term, in some cases for as long as 20 years. This is necessitated by the profound disabilities that they work with: in order to work meaningfully with their participants, they need to spend a long time getting to know them, understanding how they perceive the world, and working closely with carers and family members. They place a lot of emphasis on the people around the disabled person. They identify one achievable outcome for the project, such as someone being able to leave their seat.

Although they work with a lot of technology, they were quite critical of a lot of work that takes the opposite approach of starting with the technology rather than understanding the needs of the participant. For example, I was initially pointed towards Artlink by MAKLab [see entry below], who had collaborated with them previously on a project, but Artlink were very critical of the workshop they had run: they described how the makerspace staff were fixated with particular pieces of technology and that everything else flowed from there.

Craft more generally plays a large role in a lot of their projects: she [the representative I spoke with] described people getting "lost in the process". Often, what is made is not particularly important or even valued, but the process itself is much more important. This is especially true for people with severe autism, for example.

Specific challenges she identified included sustaining involvement, including amongst carers and family, managing expectations and identifying what it is that people want to do. They want to find gentle ways to slowly introduce new experiences, while avoiding assumptions about what people can and can't do.

She did also voice significant concerns around disabled rights in general when the topic of activism was raised. In particular, she felt that there is often a risk of catering to the more "able" disabled who are capable of voicing their requirements, which can be damaging for those with more profound disabilities.

FabLab Belfast

14th May 2015

Northern Ireland has two FabLabs, runs as partner organizations. See separate notes for FabLab Derry-Londonderry.

This Lab is sited in the Ashton Centre, a community center in Northern Belfast. The Ashton Centre is the largest employer in North Belfast, outside the public sector. This neighborhood was one of those worst affected by sectarian violence. This traumatic past is still evident in street art, and in the huge metal gates that are still padlocked every night to prevent movement between loyalist and republican neighborhoods. FabLab Belfast was located here after careful consideration, as an explicit intervention to assist community cohesion and economic regeneration. Adjacent to childcare facilities and a primary school, the Lab is bright and welcoming. It is all on the ground floor, and it proves accessible to people with a range of abilities.

FabLab Belfast shares its sister lab's rich engagement with a wealth of community activities. The emphasis is on education, raising aspiration and self-belief, encouraging individuals and communities to engage with imaginative processes. The aim is to facilitate people finding not just "new ways of doing the same thing" but to explore ways of doing new things. Working with narrative and metaphor to explain processes and conceptualize new ideas appears to be integral to the work of the lab (e.g. thinking of a laser cutter as a paintbrush). The Lab sees itself as a disruptive presence, that doesn't fit current models of peacemaking. The Lab believes that arts practice is integral to everything it does. They have a visionary quality, seeing 20 years ahead, rather than to the next election. FabLab Belfast defines itself as not fitting into existing categories. They cast themselves as enablers of the future, not just technologically, but in terms of the future of individuals and communities. Subversion was a prominent feature of our discussion. They have a great track record of working with disabled makers. One narrative, which seems particularly powerful, is of a man in a wheelchair who was amazed to be handed the hammer and invited to force the pieces together while the "expert" held the wooden joint and put himself at risk of being injured. "Handing the hammer" to the disempowered seems a powerful representation of this Lab's ethos and aspiration.

One particularly striking piece of evidence regarding the Lab's effectiveness comes in the form of a tweet (the investigator was shown a screenshot) by a young woman with mental health/learning difficulties who had been unable to attend school. After visiting the Lab and making some jewelry, she posted a tweet on the public feed, thanking the Lab staff for their help. This from a person who had not left her house for quite some time, feeling able to express her experience in public on social media.

FabLab BEC (Cockermouth)

8th May 2015

Britain's Energy Coast (http://www.britainsenergycoast.co.uk/) funds this lab. There are two premises, the West Lakes Academy at Egremont (I didn't visit this one) and in Cockermouth. This FabLab is located in a small industrial park near the town center. There is no signage (you would have to know it was there) until you reach the building itself, which is identified by the FabLab logo. There is ample parking directly outside the entrance, and most of the Lab is on the ground floor, on the same level as the street. The Lab has taken over commercial/warehouse premises. There are no evident "accessibility adaptations" to the facilities. The doors may be too narrow for some wheelchair users. Similarly, the toilets, although on the ground floor, could be too narrow. Nonetheless, a group of disabled people has been into the lab and engaged successfully with the equipment (see below).

The Cockermouth lab is designed to meet the needs of the local community, and so craft, agriculture and the nuclear industry seem to be shaping their activities and development. The emphasis seems to be on responding to local economic conditions, so "high-tech crafting", prototyping and small-business support are key elements of the offer. They are very proud of a local retired man who has adapted a 3D printer to work with clay. Entrepreneurship is a focus, with case studies about interior design and restaurant fit-outs being prominently displayed in the Lab. The rural location poses a challenge in terms of attracting users (one craft user dropped in while I was there – arrangements seem to be ad hoc and depend upon a member of staff being available to help). Word of mouth among local people seems to be the main "marketing" tool, although their website is very informative. The Lab also hosts specific interventions for schools and local groups, as well as a summer school for young people.

I visited the Wild Zucchini Bistro in Cockermouth, where most of the interior décor was created in the FabLab. I spoke to the owner, who makes a very strong case for the economic necessity of the FabLab to the development of her business. She also has a background in mental health and has some strong opinions on how the Lab should publicize itself and reach out to more users.

The Lab is not aware of any disabled users who have made use of the equipment as "individual" approaches. A session making gliders was hosted for a group with varying levels of ability. This group came into the Lab and it seems to have been a positive experience for all involved. It was organized via Sellafield's community engagement function. The Lab seems keen to work with people in this way, when structured sessions are proposed by organizations. The member of staff I spoke to was very candid about what he perceived to be a training need – that he would be happy to do more work with disabled people, but he felt unsure and out of his depth in terms of how to support users with diverse needs.

FabLab Cockermouth is clearly highly valued by those who use it. Resource issues may be one reason why its offer is not promoted more vigorously among the local community. Future funding is uncertain; prototyping and entrepreneurial support for SMEs seem to be their main focus with a second strand of activities aimed at schools and young people. There is no explicit focus on engaging with disabled users and no current strategy to do so in future. They appear to be incredibly helpful and supportive to those who approach them in search of help, but they are not in a position to seek new disabled users in a proactive manner.

FabLab Nerve Centre, Derry-Londonderry

13th May 2015

Northern Ireland has two FabLabs, runs as partner organizations. See separate notes for FabLab Belfast.

The "Nerve Centre" is in the city center, occupying a converted youth hostel in premises that have been rebuilt since the Troubles. The street outside is steep, but it would be possible to alight from a car. Entry is at street level, via automatic doors with "push pads" at a convenient height for wheelchair users. Most of the facilities are on the ground floor, although some machines are in the basement and the kitchen is upstairs. It is difficult to comment fully on accessibility because the whole lab was being refitted at the time of my visit. They are adding capacity (bigger and more numerous machines), extra kit (public address mic system so instructors can be heard) and bright new décor to make the space more welcoming. This is a Lab with a rich history and an ambitious future.

This is one of the oldest-established labs in the UK (8-10 years). Two things are particularly striking about the ethos and activities of the lab: 1. How integrally the space and its activities are embedded in community activism and 2. How the Northern Irish government sees the "maker space" as an explicit contribution to processes of peace and reconciliation and thus requested the labs to be set up, bringing over the Massachusetts Institute for Technology experts to advise on the location.

The lab boasts such breadth and depth of engagement with a whole range of users that it's difficult to pick out specifics. Many people with disabilities have engaged with the lab, but the Lab Manager stated that statistics are generally lacking, hence one of the reasons for setting up the Fab Foundation (in progress, UK-wide).

A stand-out project is the fabrication of a giant temple sculpture, which people painted with symbols and phrases before ritually setting fire to it. This seems a fascinating example of political making: "Over the course of a week, people were asked to 'leave a memory behind, let go of the past and look to the future'. Up to 60,000 visitors wrote personal messages directly on to the interior and exterior walls and pillars, and filling the inside with pictures of loved ones, handwritten messages, and symbols of peace." http://www.artichoke.uk.com/events/temple/ The Lab Manager suggests that the unique context of Northern Irish communities probably primes people to engage in critical and political making processes in a way that may not come so readily to other communities.

Recently, the Nerve Centre has taken "micro labs" out into libraries offering 2-hour interventions. The Lab Manager believes that libraries are the way forward, in his bid to "Fab-ise" community groups. One plan for future development is to create a number of neighborhood labs addressing specific needs/user groups. One of these would include a lab focused on mental health. The Lab Manager noted intellectual property and sustainability as the two greatest challenges facing the Lab's development. Nonetheless, there is such a wealth of material here that it merits a research project in its own right.

Dundee Makerspace

11th May 2015

Dundee Makerspace has been running since June 2014 and is currently located on the ground floor of a modern office building in Dundee's technology sector, alongside many of the city's computer game companies. They have around 50 members who pay £25 a month each for 24-hour access and storage, with a number of members taking a more active role in organizing the space. Much of their equipment is scavenged or bought second hand, but they have also invested in large pieces of equipment like laser cutters. They emerged from Dundee's software society, and this is reflected in their membership.

At this stage, their membership is still very much made up of "typical" makerspace users. Like other smaller spaces, there is a strong emphasis on community, peer support and collaborative learning. They provide a space and some facilities that would be impractical for members to own privately, but limited services beyond this. They have no staff members, so their ability to do outreach or marketing is very limited. Most new members come to them through their regular Monday night open session or find them through Facebook or word of mouth. Many people come along with a specific problem that they want to address and are either using the space's membership as a sort of "hive mind", or want help developing skills.

At this point, they have not had any usage by disabled users. They are funded as a social enterprise, and other funded organizations have expressed interest in using the space for therapeutic purposes, e.g. with cancer patients and people with learning difficulties, but this has not panned out yet. They were enthusiastic about the idea of DIY assistive technology, but felt they knew little about this area—however, if a disabled person were to come in with a specific problem, they felt that the challenge would be tackled with gusto.

They do run events in the space for the wider public, some of which have been well attended by people outside their normal user base. This includes an open weekend that was attended by many parents and children and a Robot Wars event. The space is also used by similar organizations to host talks and workshops, and by wildly different organizations—recent events have included morning dance sessions and hairdressing lessons.

The space is quite accessible, being on the ground floor, and the space is large and open. Parking is available. The only difficulty would be the main doors and two interior doors to reach the space, which are manual. However, there is 24-hour security at the front desk who could help with this.

FabLab Ellesmere Port

29th April 2015

FabLab Ellesmere Port is the sister lab to FabLab Manchester. As with Manchester, it is run as a charitable enterprise by The Manufacturing Institute. This is a relatively new lab (opened October 2013). It was set up at the invitation of the local council, to help address social, learning and skills needs in the local area. It is believed to be unique in the UK, in that it's literally "on the high street" – a shop front premises, integrated into the town center, and attracting lots of "drop in" social users or just curious passers-by.

There is a clear mission to integrate with other local organizations with the collective aim of building personal confidence, offering social opportunities, and addressing skills gaps with both child and adult learners. The Lab is a key element of the "Wellbeing Highstreet" initiative, working with a local group called SEED. Activities include supporting a community farm – during the winter, farm users will come to the lab to make or repair tools, and to make Christmas cards to sell as a revenue stream.

The Lab has a very wide range of users. They are currently looking at ways of documenting users and their "journeys" more formally. They are not aware of any particular group being excluded, but there are examples of individuals excluding themselves due to anticipated difficulties (e.g. language barriers). Friday and Saturday drop-in sessions are busy and sociable. Some people don't make anything but enjoy the atmosphere and the open kitchen. Others are long-term users, some of whom the Lab staff are trying to signpost to entrepreneurial opportunities, although the makers themselves aren't always aware of their own potential. There are good links with business start-up funding and support, to refer people on to appropriate mentorship. Most users make practical aids. Arts and crafts makers actually have difficulties using the equipment creatively!

The Lab staff are aware of two users with disabilities, both of whom would make inspiring case studies. The first is a woman with mobility difficulties who started from no knowledge at all, and now makes ambitious aids, including a cover for her mobility scooter. Both she and her husband are registered disabled. The second is a D/deaf user who is making bunk beds for his children. Communication is an issue, but he has developed a working relationship with a specific staff member.

The Lab's main outreach and events programs are focused on education. They are part of a successful adult education course with a local college and they also do a lot of work with schools, supporting teachers as well as students. They report some students changing their GCSE options to include Design after their Lab experience. They're aiming to secure sponsorship with multinationals including Vauxhall and Esso to produce the apprentices of the future.

They have no planned or existing projects focusing specifically on disability, but they seem to be attracting disabled people anyway. The building is generally accessible (having been a Council building and recently refurbished). It is all on one level, open plan, with accessible toilets. The kitchen is a standard set-up which may not be accessible to everyone, but staff are always on hand to help. In fact, the staff are evidently welcoming and supportive, and highly motivated to provide an inclusive environment. The only practical difficulty is accessing the building from the car park (which has lots of spaces) but is behind the shop front and requires quite a long route over rough ground. They are seeking funding to build ramps to the back door, which would address the only apparent access issue.

FabLab Exeter

2nd February 2015

The FabLab opened in May 2014 and is housed in the newly refurbished library of Exeter City Council. The premises are fully accessible, there is a 1 in 12 ramp outside, zero thresholds and ground floor access. There are 5 disabled parking bays outside.

The funding was mainly by the council, with additional support from the global innovation foundation NESTA/Nominet, and a local charity called Real Ideas. This latter charity is focused upon those aged 18 or under. There is a commitment to set up satellite centers in sixth form colleges and 5 laptops have been purchased to assist in fulfilling this. The Exeter lab subscribes to the FabLab Charter and is established as a Community Interest Company. There are some 25 volunteers and there is the intention to create a membership scheme though at present the FabLab is not fully open to members.

Some staff had in-depth knowledge of disabilities, with one staff member having undertaken research into social perceptions of hidden disabilities as part of her degree course and another with a background in architectural practice majoring in disability access. The Lab's vision was born out of the

Head of Library Services' aspiration to see libraries take on new functions. The aim is to upskill and educate the community in terms of digital making.

The Lab has been running 1-hour taster courses mainly for schools. There have been some expressions of interest from some local charities, e.g. a charity supporting ADHD wishing to visit. A local specialist College has been in conversation about Lab use by one of their math classes. Royal Devon and Exeter Hospital have proposed making an adaption for people's hands, including bespoke hand controls, e.g. joystick for wheelchairs. Objects on display in the Lab included a "shark skin" prototype to test how wind travels over a building, and a hinge for a shower. Planned outreach activities included a talk to Exeter Chamber of Commerce.

It is necessary to pre-register to use the Lab. Impressions of user demographics suggest that people engaging with the Lab already have an interest in making things. Although staff caution that it is too early to specify types of users and they are currently developing the Lab's offer, they observe that users are 2:1 male to female. One volunteer has early onset dementia due to Parkinson's disease, another is red-green color blind. Staff members discussed the importance of finding different ways of using language.

The website has just been relaunched by the city council, but it was felt that the Library was not well signposted. There is a lack of awareness at present, though a major PR campaign about the council's services is planned, including the FabLab facility. Interestingly, staff here mentioned MAKLab [see entry below] in Glasgow as an example of best practice for its good location, provision of incubator spaces and use by students.

FabLab Falmouth

3rd February 2015

The lab is in an accessible building at Falmouth University, Penryn campus. The facility subscribes to the FabLab Charter. There is an accessible toilet close by; the building is served with disabled parking bays.

The FabLab was funded through European Social Fund money and has been open to students and the public for around 18 months. The funding is due to expire in the summer of this year. The FabLab was the brainchild of the autonomic research group. Its vision is the digital application of design and craft. A lab manager is dedicated to being in the lab 1.5 days a week, with two technicians offering technical support to users for 3 days a week. Users tend to be PhD students – more from Exeter than Falmouth, as they jointly share the campus; and independent microbusinesses who used the facility for small scale runs or first stage prototypes. There is an emphasis on product development over artistic expression. For example, one engineer came into the Lab and taught himself Computer-Aided Design, while another designed and printed an automatic lifting machine for his Aga [stove]. The lab manager felt a key measure of his success would be repeat visitors.

The facility is advertised via social media and the university website, but it is not open in the evenings or at weekends. The aim is to create some ongoing training following induction sessions of 2-2.5 hours. Possibly three sessions are needed to become competent with the milling machine. Capacity must be managed carefully, as the FabLab can accommodate no more than 4 people at once. Taster sessions have been held with the "Makeshift do" for the local craft council. Some 100 people had attended inductions on using the equipment. A business assist program helped business start-ups. The university has an outreach program with an integrated social media campaign, developing an access model for the facility and an entry point. A question lab staff posed was clarifying the purpose of the Lab, and FabLabs more generally: "is the purpose to produce a breakthrough design and product, or to raise awareness through show and tell?"

Lab staff had a long connection with the FabLab movement. While they noted the utopianism around FabLabs, they emphasized their strong belief in the importance of promoting understanding of how things are made, and the value of design. One anecdotal example included a friend who had designed and invented his own barcode reading device so that he could do the stocktaking at the hardware store where he worked. Staff noted that "Arduino [open source electronics] units resolving digital interaction are likely to develop successfully and push boundaries".

The facility is not specifically promoted to disabled people though neither is there any attempt to discourage access. The staff mentioned a ten-year-old boy who had attended the lab with his blind father and a small business that had designed an extension to a long cane. The Lab hosts the Remap project, which involves people with skills in engineering solving problems with assistive technology. There is also a Royal Society of Arts project, connecting people with digital fabrication skills to people with disabilities who wanted assistive technologies developed. Lab staff felt that there was no exemplar FabLab working with disabled people. However, the Barcelona FabLab was cited as being particularly innovative and community-focused.

FabLab Enginuity (Ironbridge)

7th May 2015

This FabLab is located within the Enginuity visitor attraction, a constituent of the Ironbridge Museums complex, drawing on the industrial heritage of this region in central England. Part of the National Design and Technology Centre, the Lab is one year old and already has a track record of engaging special needs groups from local schools. Designed to engage children and young people, the building is filled with technology-related exhibits which invite visitors to get "hands on". The attraction as a whole sees 100,000 visitors a year, although many will pass through the public exhibits without engaging with the lab. The whole space is noisy [which may pose issues for people with autism, for example], but it also feels accessible, vibrant and filled with activity.

The FabLab is managed and funded by the Ironbridge Gorge Museums Trust, which manages several museums and heritage sites within the Shropshire area. This is a new lab, set within a purpose-built visitor attraction. It therefore has lifts, accessible toilets and good access routes into the building. The Lab itself sits on a mezzanine floor, suspended above the main visitor attraction. There is a lift as well as stairs. Fabricated gates and railings prevent unsupervised access. These gates are low enough for wheelchair users and children to see over into the making space. The "fences" are brightly colored, and easily opened to allow people into the space. In addition to bespoke sessions for schools, the Lab runs an open-access booking system, and has volunteers present as well as paid staff.

The focus of the Lab is on educational activity, achieved mainly via engagement with local schools. Ages range from primary school upwards. They work with children on STEAM (Science Technology Engineering Arts and Math) projects – they are keen to emphasize the "arts" content within the STEM subject focus. They have done some work with a local artist on potential uses of the equipment in a craft context. The Lab works with large employers, including Jaguar Landrover [international automobile manufacturer], with the aim of inspiring the "employees of tomorrow".

The Lab defines itself as "independent" (although it is part of the FabLab network), and so it has some extra kit, such as heat presses, in addition to the standard Lab specifications. While the focus is very much on educational interventions with young people, a range of community users exists and demand for access to the open sessions is high. Present during my visit was a volunteer who is a retired engineer.

Lab staff spoke enthusiastically about a young person referred to the Lab by his care-worker, as part of his rehabilitation process. The Lab thinks of him as a great success story. The young person is now a regular user and is beginning to develop personal skills and confidence as he starts to train others. 50-400 people per day may engage with the Lab in some way. Numbers are limited by capacity issues. The need for multiple machines and the "scalability" of the resources is evident. Timed ticket sessions are pre-booked in advance. While accessibility and ease of movement around the lab are generally good (there are lots of work benches and various teaching spaces), some equipment is too high for wheelchair users to reach. The CNC router is loud and dangerous. A solution is being developed which involves "live streaming" the hazardous machines in action from a safer location. Wi-Fi throughout the building will allow processes to be shown on LCD screens in the main space, attracting the attention of more visitors. Alternative means of accessibility also include a projector, which allows live software tutorials, and the installation of smart boards for teaching.

Enginuity is located in a rural setting; a small village with brown "tourist signs" guiding people to the attraction. Several bus routes serve the attraction and there is ample parking, some of it reserved for Blue Badge holders. There is a cafe facility in the building, which sells refreshments, but people are also welcome to bring their own food. Sofas and a range of seating are offered. Changes to this space, to make it more welcoming and accessible, were made in response to feedback from special needs groups.

MAKE Aberdeen

17th March 2015

MAKE Aberdeen is a joint venture between Peacock Visual Arts and Aberdeen City Council, which had operated in commercial premises in the city center for just over a year. Their main goal is to provide people with access to equipment that they wouldn't otherwise have access to.

Attendees include everyone from art students to people working in the oil industry. As with MAKLab [see below], they find that 3D printers are usually the hook that draws people in, but laser cutting proves to be much more useful for most people. MAKE offers annual membership or a day rate for access. This provides one-on-one tuition to help turn ideas into reality.

Usage is incredibly varied, from costume making to electronics. There were many examples of people using the facilities to support business or entrepreneurship: this included people making jewelry to sell at arts fairs and inventors who came in looking for help turning their technical drawings into prototypes. This, in particular, would have been a stumbling block for them if MAKE had not existed. Equally, lots of people just make things for the joy of it. They also have film-making equipment and run animation workshops and help people document their making.

They have at least two members with physical disabilities, but this has not proven to be an issue. Accessing the standing laser cutters is the only real concern. The projects these users engage in were not related to their disabilities. No real adaptations have been necessary, and staff were unsure about how this might be dealt with in the future if issues arose. As the Lab is a council and arts charity venture, located on council premises, a lot of thought has been given to accessibility. Doors were widened (but are all manual) and a stairlift has been installed, with all staff trained in its operation. Disabled toilets are present.

MAKE do a lot of outreach activities. Two workshops a week are run to introduce groups to the space, which has included school classes and community groups. These have included groups of people with autism, and in the future, they have plans to work on projects that relate specifically to their autism. They have ambitions to set up a mobile site in a mobile library and have discussed this with Aberdeenshire Council.

They also do work placements for unemployed people. People on placement are required to help with general cleaning and maintenance, but they also get trained up on all the machines. Although there have not been any big success stories yet, staff are hopeful that the skills being provided will be useful to local employers, including the oil industry. MAKE would like to do more outreach, but with only two members of staff, this is difficult. They hope to secure funding to do more in the future.

MAKLab Glasgow

11th March 2015

MAKLab is a well-established and ambitious makerspace in Glasgow, which has been in operation for three years. The site is in commercial premises towards the West of the City Centre. MAKLab is a charity and social enterprise aiming to make digital technology as widely available at the lowest cost possible.

The type of person using the space is constantly evolving. They get design students and people running businesses, but also a lot of people who are just "tinkerers". They get a lot of people who believe they are not technical or not creative, but who are able to unlock these skills. People joining are typically attracted by the 3D printers but often find that other equipment is more useful. In addition to obvious makerspace equipment, MAKLab also have a new textiles area. This is reaching a different set of users, but also creating new links between this area and traditional makerspace activities. For tinkerers it's more of a creative outlet.

The projects being undertaken are equally varied. Some people run entire businesses out of the space, e.g. someone who sells model kits to model makers. Other people have an idea they want to test out and this allows them to do that instead of having prototypes made in China. Staff were not aware of any current users with physical disabilities, and they expect that this is partly due to lack of accessibility and also because they're not well-known enough. However, a number of members had children or teens with disabilities, including autism, that they brought along and tried to engage in activities.

Tasks tend not to be related to their children's disability but were more about bringing young people to a creative space.

However, MAKLab's outreach activities are wide-ranging and ambitious, with commercial activities supporting their outreach angle. They have set up branches in a museum and high school, with another forthcoming in a library. The library, in particular, is socially focused. Most of their equipment can be packed up and taken out in a van, but they also have a space downstairs that can be used for events. No two outreach events are the same, and they typically work with organizations who come to them with requests to facilitate workshops.

In relation to disability, MAKLab have recently joined the e-NABLE network, a worldwide organization putting maker spaces in touch with people who need prosthetics, especially children. Prosthetics are printed from scratch in the locality of the end user, but customized online, with people all over the world contributing to improving open-source designs. As a rule, MAKLab is less interested in doing this for people in need of prosthetics, and more interested in giving them the skills to build what they want. MAKLab have also done work with ArtLink developing tools for work with adults with profound learning disabilities who wouldn't normally be able to take part in group activities.

MAKLab are very aware of accessibility problems, particularly the lack of accessible toilets and stairs without lift. They are looking to get funding to fix this. Otherwise, the accessibility was quite good. They have another space for "dirty" making that is trickier, as much of the equipment requires standing and physical exertion.

FabLab Plymouth at Plymouth College of Art

2nd February 2015

The FabLab is on the ground floor of the college in a large room and fully wheelchair accessible. The building is served by an accessible toilet and 3 disabled parking bays. The Lab subscribes to the UK FabLabs charter.

The Lab is quite new, having opened to college students in August 2014 and to the public in November 2014. The presence of a vinyl cutter still in its box indicates how new this provision is. The lab has one volunteer and opens to the public from 2 pm to 9 pm Thursdays and every alternate Saturday. Friday is set aside for the business sector. The lab is used by students 50% of the time. The Lab manager explained that: "the lab is split between supporting students and one day supporting business; the focus is on curriculum, community and commerce." Members of the public only pay for materials.

The Lab's vision is for the public to be digitally skilled. The Lab manager also spoke eloquently of the role of the FabLab in supporting the renewal of traditional industrial skills such as glass making: "We can make skills and craft skills relevant to society. We can use the FabLab to make molds for the sustainable glass furnace." Hence the facility is part of the arts and crafts provision of the college. The Lab manager was positive about people using open-access online resources to support self-learning. Outreach activity had included a Saturday arts club and advertising in newspapers. However, Lab staff expected early pioneers to be experts in their fields and artists. Provision appears focused on artists and designers, with a new course launching for professionals, and a talk being delivered to the Crafts Council. Lab staff stressed the importance of design: "teach them [lab users] how to design and what goes into the machines."

Again, this Lab was engaged with the e-NABLE movement and showed a prosthetic hand that had been printed for a little girl following a story in a local newspaper.

Westhill Men's Shed

22nd May 2015

Westhill Men's Shed is a workshop and communal area utilized mostly by retired men in the Westhill area, which has been fully open since 2013. Men's Sheds originated in 1996 in Australia, aiming to address issues of mental health and wellbeing amongst men, particularly those who have retired. Mental health is a huge and largely unacknowledged problem for this population, who may face a crisis of identity and loneliness once they have stopped working. They are generally also hesitant to discuss these issues, fearing the stigma attached to it. Westhill is the flagship shed of the Scottish Men's Shed Association, which now has some 13 sheds, many of them across Aberdeenshire.

The shed is located in a disused library and contains a (non-digital) workshop comprising benches and large pieces of machinery such as lathes. There are around 50 core members, but thousands of visitors pass through the shed each year. However, most of the activity takes place in the social area outside the workshop, which has couches, tables, a pool table, dart board and tea/coffee facilities. When I visited, there were at least a dozen people in this space and only one or two in the workshop. In fact, many people don't use the workshop at all, but come to socialize or play bridge. Several men recovering from strokes come in to practice speaking. Other members run cooking workshops to help those whose spouses/partners have died, and who consequently struggle to look after themselves.

The shed is entirely self-funding. Members earn money by selling the things they have made, performing small jobs for clients and by upcycling tools and hardware that they can sell on. The only thing they can't cover is rent, and the building is provided for free by the council. They operate as a social enterprise, and certain members act as Chairman, etc., but they have a strictly flat hierarchy. The Scottish association, which has only one funded staff member, mostly served to bootstrap new sheds and support them. It is important that the men take ownership of the shed and run it themselves.

The benefits seen by shed users are astounding. Analysis has shown that investments made in the shed show a tenfold return in terms of social and healthcare costs. Many of the men find they are healthier because of being happier, and as a result can scale back their medication. I spoke to one regular, a 90-year-old WW2 veteran, who repeatedly said that the shed had "changed his life" after his wife passed away.

In a lot of ways, the Men's Shed has a lot in common with some of the less commercial makerspaces I visited, which were as much about community as they were about making. However, by making this more explicit and by not fixating on particular technologies or activities, they have been able to have an appeal that most of these makerspaces can only dream of.

Summary and analysis

With the exception of one prominent makerspace based in the Northeast of England, who declined our request for a visit on the basis that they had too many researchers making demands on their time, the makerspaces we approached were unfailingly helpful and positive. The project team would like to thank all the makerspace staff and volunteers who went out of their way to be so helpful, giving freely of their time and expertise.

This initial scoping exercise generated an extraordinarily rich and voluminous body of material, much of which remains to be analyzed in detail. Clearly, further research around makerspace culture and provision is needed. Early work by Sabine Hielscher and Adrian Smith, for example, suggests that analyzing the processes and products of community making spaces might "require a portfolio of theoretical resources to make sense of this activity" (2014, 25). Furthermore, they remind us that the diverse perspectives of the three researchers involved in the survey require investigators "to be reflexive about their own interpretations of practitioners' activities (and normative research goals), considering that they can play a role in shaping and representing such activities" (51). From our survey, we can draw the following initial insights:

Resource and sustainability

Funding is almost always an issue. Many FabLabs have industry or university backing, which helps them operationally but influences strongly who can access them, for what and when. Short term grants and uncertainty about sustainability mean that makerspaces are often in rented accommodation, can move at short notice (the Greater Manchester FabLabs, for example, have been dramatically reconfigured during the lifetime of this project), and are therefore not always able to implement structural adaptations that would make their premises more physically accessible. Pressure on resources also means that paid staff, if present, are often part-time and/or on shorter-term contracts. Most makerspaces rely on volunteers. These constraints mean that many makerspaces cannot afford to market themselves, or in fact do not wish to publicize their offer for fear of being overwhelmed by demand. Generally, notwithstanding focused outreach projects, members of the public accessing makerspaces will already be familiar with making culture and have some technical experience with the equipment. Any makerspace signing up to the FabLab charter must offer free public access sessions, but these can be crowded, noisy, and filled with people who seem to know what they are doing. Staff and volunteers may not have time to support a complete beginner into the making process. Such factors could, unintentionally, combine to discourage a disabled would-be maker.

Inclusion and diversity

Makerspace cultures are by definition open, sharing, and focused on problem-solving. Some of the makerspace staff with whom we spoke could point to examples of disabled people engaging and making in their labs. A disabled woman had fabricated a bespoke shelter for her mobility scooter, because she had nowhere to store it in her house. A D/deaf man and his son had refitted their caravan. Some disabled people were now volunteering to help others into the maker community. However, these examples were completely anecdotal rather than formally documented, and pointed to exceptionally determined individuals whose achievements were few and far between. These findings resonate with what G. Thomas Couser observes, in which dominant social narratives position disabled individuals with "stories worth telling" as exceptional individuals or "supercrips" who overcome personal tragedy through sheer force of will in order to succeed in the ableist world (2001, 78-79). Dominant social narratives set an unfortunate precedent, then, implying that "ordinary" disabled people are simply not trying hard enough to live up to these inspiring examples, and draws attention away from the important work of identifying and critiquing the disabling social structures that underpin such positionings. Just because exceptionally determined and resourceful individuals did manage to access makerspaces successfully, it does not mean that other disabled people could be expected to find a route to doing the same. Further research, analysis and awareness-raising are needed, particularly as we found that resource issues prevented most makerspaces from monitoring the demographics of their users – again, a further piece of research is needed here. Several makerspace staff confided that they did not feel disability confident and would not how to support someone with particular needs if that person had attended without their own supporter.

Conclusion

The democratization and personalization of manufacturing raise profound questions about intellectual property and economic models, leading some to hail the "maker" movement as the dawning of a new industrial revolution (Gershenfeld 2005; 2012; Lau, Mitani and Igarashi, 2012). Such claims, however, require a critical appraisal. In their 2017 article "The Logic of Digital Utopianism" Sascha Dickel and Jan-Felix Schrape identify naively optimistic narratives in current media coverage, which seem to suggest that 3D printers will solve all of our problems. It is true that disrupting the traditional roles of producer and consumer has radical potential. This is particularly so for disabled people who might, for example, benefit from the e-NABLE network supplying prosthetic limbs. But in general, current makerspace provision tends to privilege the affluent, technically adept maker and risks the exclusion of many groups and individuals.

Auto-ethnographer Selena Nemorin, for example, documents the frustrations of working with the technical restrictions of currently available 3D printers. She uses the phrase "mediated alienation" to describe the practical difficulties inherent in the claim that 3D printers can materialize thoughts: "My labour [sic] in this setting was controlled by digital rules set by an external entity with the power to dictate how I was able to embody myself through what I made" (2016, 18). Nemorin's experience seems to suggest that, far from opening new possibilities for self-expression, the practical restrictions of currently available 3D printers (rather than their utopian future capabilities) may close down, dictate, and discourage.

Laura Devendorf and her co-researchers offer a post-humanist critique of these potentially limiting qualities. Difficulties like those experienced by Nemorin arise because 3D printers are designed on anthropocentric terms, framing "the human maker as the locus of innovation and creativity and their building materials as passive receptors or container for makers' ideas" (Devendorf et al. 2016, 172). In short, you are what you print. If the print goes awry, it's because of a failure in the maker. We found that challenging ideas about what a successful 3D print might be was essential to managing experiences of failure for the participants in our project. Inherent in the operation of 3D printers for the consumer market is the assumption that accuracy of replication is the primary goal and, where this does not happen, the print is seen to have "failed." Conventionally, the competence of a maker is judged by their ability to coax the machine into faultless replication of the virtual design. The primary goal is: "fidelity to the original digital model" (Ibid.). When fidelity is lost in the process of translating data into things, the human maker is framed as unsuccessful. Managing the "affective labour of failing" (Nemorin 2016, 1) became particularly pressing in our project, working with novice makers who were already starting from a socially-defined position of lack.

This is not to say that disabled people are excluded entirely from the maker movement. Some early adopters have been at the forefront of developing their own customized practical aids. The e-NABLE network, for example, connects makers with people who need prosthetic hands. Cynthia Bennett and her co-researchers have begun to explore how the making of 3D printed prosthetic limbs relates to the construction of self and the "development of ability identity" (2016, 1746). However, e-NABLE and other networks largely reproduce the boundaries between expert makers and the disabled recipients of that skill: "women and minorities are underrepresented" in making communities, while questions remain about how "people with disabilities begin to be recognized as makers" (Bennett et al. 2016, 1748).

Researchers, facilitators and collaborators involved with "In the Making" chose to situate the project as addressing the question of how disabled people might recast themselves as makers of their own solutions. The enabling factor in our collaborators' achievements was the co-evolution of what Devendorf and her colleagues identify as a post-anthropocentric maker space, "challenging norms around what it means to be a 'maker'" (2016, 171). Initially, some of our facilitators were alarmed by the de-hierarchized space in which disabled people, often accompanied by their own machines, prostheses, and assistance animals, improvised accessible modes of making. Those instructors used to more conventional making environments were challenged to recalibrate their perceptions of what constitutes legitimate making practices. Together, facilitators and collaborators evolved approaches which "de-emphasize precision in order to make space for new ideas, forms and experiences to emerge" (Devendorf et al. 2016, 175).

However, it was not just a matter of sitting people in front of the equipment and saying, "Go ahead, make something that speaks about your life." Being offered access to technology that can, subject to practical restrictions, "make anything" can be overwhelming: "that idea of saying 'make whatever you want' is quite a frightening thing" (Armson 2015, n.

pag.). Our project needed to generate a process for negotiating these complex issues within the inclusive FabLab. Chapter 3 unfolds our co-constructed solutions for inclusive making practices.

Take-aways

- Our project visited a diverse range of makerspaces across the UK to try to find out more about current usage by disabled people.
- Makerspaces are hugely varied, but their unifying ethos is one of open access, sharing expertise, and focus on problem-solving.
- Constraints on resources mean that many makerspaces encounter challenges around sustainability, accessible premises and staffing. Such constraints can unintentionally exclude disabled people and novice makers. People need support to overcome these barriers.
- Anecdotally, disabled people are accessing makerspaces and using technology to make things that they want or need. Further research, analysis and awareness-raising are needed, particularly as we found that resource issues prevented most makerspaces from monitoring the demographics of their users.
- Unrealistic media narratives about 3D printing might serve to discourage diverse makers from approaching the technology. Preconceptions around valid making practices, and what constitutes a successful outcome, need to be unpacked and opened to debate, in order to manage experiences of failure.
- Makerspace staff expressed a training need around how to support disabled makers.

Chapter 3

Getting Started

Let's begin with the magic box:

This box can make anything that you can imagine.
Think it, and it will materialise inside the box.
What's in the box?

Share with a partner. As you listen to your partner's account, think about the story behind the object. What is the need, desire or experience that prompted them to imagine their object?

(Ideation prompt, field work, 2015)

To many people, particularly those unfamiliar with the technology, a 3D printer can seem like a magic box. Entry-level machines are mainly hollow cubes, occupying two to three cubic feet on a tabletop. Once they are supplied with a design code, they appear to materialise objects out of thin air, transforming data into things. Within technical limitations, they can make anything we can think: "the formerly fictional idea of such a 'magic machine' has been turned into reality" (Walter-Herrmann and Büching 2013, 10). While we have not yet reached the realms of the *Star Trek* replicator, Bryan Nelson (2015) claims that digital fabrication technologies are developing towards such capabilities.

The purpose of this inquiry is not to explore science fiction, but to consider 3D printing technologies as they currently exist, and how they might offer opportunities to people who may be excluded from or discouraged by more traditional forms of making practice. A 3D printer is only as effective as the design it has been programmed to print. The first stage in a 3D printing workshop is therefore to generate ideas for things to print. The technology is productive when it is driven by the imaginations of its users. The inclusive fabrication workshops were therefore designed to nurture the imaginative and creative contributions of our participants. Inevitably different workshops evolved along different paths to accommodate the expressed needs of participants, but the basic principles were adhered to throughout. Below I reproduce the standard workshop schedule, as it was sent out to participants:

Dear Fab Pioneer,

We are delighted that you have chosen to join our digital fabrication workshop at the Swinton Gateway on 25 and 26 November. You can find more information about the location and accessibility of the venue here: https://www.salford.gov.uk/swintongateway.htm

To help you get the most out of the sessions, here is some more detail about how to prepare and what to expect when you get there:

Both days run from 10 am to 3 pm, with an hour's break for lunch, 12-1. The first day will be all about finding ideas, thinking creatively and exploring our needs and aspirations. We will not begin using the 3D printers immediately – first, we will spend some time thinking about what we might wish to make. This day will be facilitated by arthur+martha: http://www.arthur-and-martha.co.uk/ To help you get the most from this day, please have a look at the attached document [below].

On the afternoon of the first day, we will be joined by an expert from FabLab Manchester, who will help us to think about how our creative ideas might translate into digital outputs, such as 3D prints.

Our second day is facilitated by Joe MacLeod-Iredale, a product designer who will help us to begin working with 3D design software. Absolutely no prior experience is necessary, and we have some project laptops with a variety of accessible mice/keyboards but, if possible, ***please bring your own laptop or tablet*** *– it may be easier to work on your own device, and you can save your designs for future reference. If you'd like to have a look at the software that we'll be using, then please download Sketchup, which is free to access here: http://www.sketchup.com/ Go ahead and play – there are lots of online tutorials and helpful hints.*

We have two 3D printers from www.ultimaker.com and they will be running throughout our workshop. The printing process can take several hours, depending upon the complexity of your object – we'll try to make sure that everyone gets to print something, but we may need to make follow-up arrangements for anything large or complex. For some ideas on what's possible, have a look at this online community: https://www.youmagine.com/

Finally, on a practical note, we can pay for your travel and associated access costs. Where the sum exceeds a few pounds, we will have to repay you via the University finance department, meaning that we will need your bank details and national insurance number.

We can offer light refreshments (soft drinks and biscuits) but our budget cannot stretch to full catering, so please either bring your own lunch or be prepared to buy it from nearby shops/cafes. If food costs will pose a challenge, then please speak to us and we'll do our best to help.

We hope that you find the experience enjoyable and inspiring. Please do not hesitate to get in touch, should you have any further questions.

Very best wishes,
The Project Team

However, as the following field notes attest, our best-laid plans did not run smoothly, with both predictable and unforeseen challenges arising. The first extract illustrates the difficulty that project participants encountered in accepting the invitation to create, pointing to the challenges inherent in supporting marginalized people to engage with an emergent technology.

Excerpt from "In the Making" project field notes:

A weekday late morning, in a design workshop in a cafe in Salford, UK. The workshop participants appear apprehensive. They know that they are going to be invited to generate ideas. Many avoid eye contact. There is a sense of fidgety discomfort.

"I'm just not creative," repeats one young woman, defensively.

"Well, don't look at me," laughs an older man, nervously.

The facilitator begins a gentle exercise, asking people to select an object from a purse or pocket and to tell someone else the story of its significance.

"Oh, I can't tell stories," says the young woman. "It'll be boring!"

Gradually, each participant feels comfortable enough to share the story of his or her object. The narratives are skillfully crafted. People delight in the accounts by their peers. Several stories are about keys to cars or front doors. Their owners speak eloquently about freedom, choice, independence, and the offer of a sanctuary to which one can return after doing battle with the world beyond. The young woman tells of her dog's name-tag, which she carries in her purse since the chain broke. She becomes animated as she speaks about the dog, its antics, what it means to her emotionally. She shows photos on her phone.

The following day, on selecting objects to print, this young woman is decided – she will design and print a new name tag for her dog. Assisted by the technical facilitator, she creates a design with 3D hearts and the name, Jorgie, in relief. When offered a choice of color to print the object, she selects a bright pink filament. Figure 3.1 shows her design, followed by figure 3.2, which captures the design emerging from the printhead:

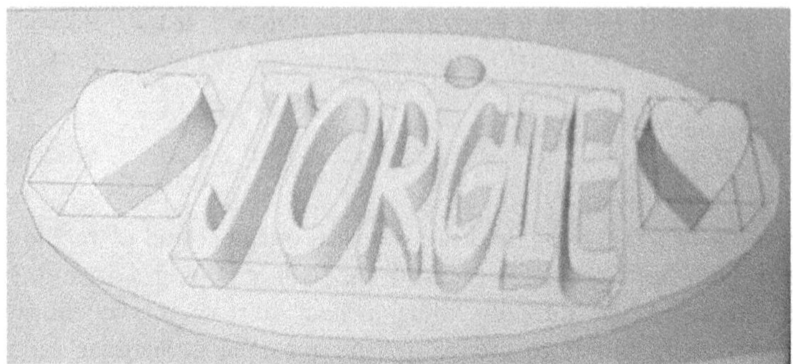

Figure 3.1. Design for a dog tag, created by a project participant.

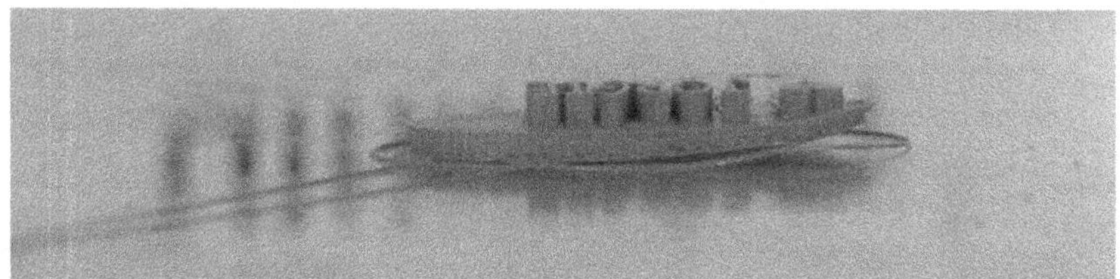

Figure 3.2. The design materializing on the print bed.

The design takes a few trial prints before it emerges accurately. The 3D printer is not entirely reliable and there can be glitches in the translation from software to object, such as omitting the heart on the left-hand side of the design. As seen in Figure 3.2, the heart is missing. The object's designer is anxious and disappointed by these problems. She says it doesn't matter, "it was silly anyway".

Eventually the technical facilitator identifies the problem and a perfect version prints. The object's designer is clearly delighted with her creation. The facilitators share her pleasure in having created such a vibrant and meaningful object. But, as she shows the new dog tag to her peers, she becomes dismissive, saying: "It's only a dog tag. What a shame I couldn't make anything useful!" The workshop facilitators reassure her that "the object is valuable because it is unique". It expresses the emotional value of her relationship with her pet dog. But she goes home appearing to judge herself harshly in relation to her making activity and its value.

September 2015, Salford, UK.

This excerpt is representative of multiple occasions during our mobile FabLab sessions when the making process highlighted the internalized narratives that appear to have profound negative effects on the perceived agency of disabled people. This young woman was quick to judge and belittle her own achievements before anyone else had the opportunity to do so.

A review of the literature around creativity and who gets to access and attribute value to creative activity, offers a clear explanation for this kind of self-diminishment, which was something we encountered again and again with our project participants, and worked hard to counter. Phelps asserts that "Creativity and innovativeness are properties that have come to be defined largely by elites through theoretical claims which reflect imaginings of their own social worth" (2012, 268). Those who are not identified with, or do not identify themselves with the creative elites who produce and define "culture", such as people high on the "deprivation index" and/or with disabilities, for example, may not consider themselves worthy participants in "creative" activities.

A body of psychological research supports "the generally accepted belief that self-confidence and creativity are positively related" (Goldsmith and Matherly 1988, 57). The core traits identified by psychologists as being associated with creativity are "independence, self-confidence and a view of oneself as creative" (Goldsmith and Matherly 1988, 47). The characteristics of the creative person are described by Stein as "self-assertive, dominant, aggressive, self-sufficient ... [he or she] leads or possesses initiative" (cited by Goldsmith and Matherly 1988, 48). While this definition of a creative person is debatable, such qualities are likely to be less common in people experiencing marginalization, and/or disabling circumstances. As a route to fostering the development of creative individuals, our project found that people can be equipped with techniques which "give permission" to be creative and see themselves as cultural producers by supporting them to overcome anxieties about creative production. This approach, however, requires reimagining creativity as something accessible to all rather than innate to particular individuals: "any activity can be done in novel ways with creative intentions" (Silvia et al. 2014, 187). Activities which were framed as "Creative" with a capital "C" were counterproductive, with the weight of expectation deterring people from engaging for fear of failure.

Reconceptualizing creativity can help encourage people outside so-called "Creative" identities (such as owning "talent" or naming oneself as an "artist") to consider themselves as having creative potential. Symons argues for perceiving creativity as "an adaptive and productive process working towards a tangible goal" (Symons 2016, 3). In an earlier piece of research that I conducted with my colleague, drama practitioner Szilvia Naray-Davey, we framed creativity as a procedure that individuals can learn to "consciously manage and successfully reproduce" (Naray-Davey and Hurley 2014, 4). If people see themselves as creative in their day-to-day lives, then they are more likely to imagine themselves as having the potential to produce creative work. There is a considerable body of research emphasizing everyday creativity (see for example Richards 2007, Su 2009, Barron 1969, Ingold and Hallam 2007, Leach 2002). These authors focus on everyday activity as creative – "with our everyday creativity, we adapt flexibly, we improvise, and we try different options, whether we are raising our child, counselling a friend, fixing our home, or planning a fundraising event" (Richards 2007, 26). Developed mainly by psychologists and anthropologists, these texts argue for recognition of oneself and others as inherently creative individuals. The challenge for our project was to translate these theoretical insights into the practical experience of a varied and diverse group of participants.

Anxieties about failure obstructed people's ability to engage with creative activities and the methods we used to overcome these issues. Furthermore, a legacy relationship with university academics and other government representatives had produced a level of distrust within our collaborator communities. Our aim was to reshape perceptions and self-perceptions of disabled people by demonstrating their creative and productive potential. The key challenge for the project was tackling decades of diminishment and negative attitudes about disabled people which affected our participants' confidence. We found that once people tackled and overcame the idea stimulation phase, engagement in the design and development process was enthusiastic.

The politics of failure

Western industrialized nations generally reproduce paradigms of educational and employment histories which teach citizens that failure is something to be avoided. Failing an exam or a test can have disastrous consequences for future success. It affects people's ability to get into their preferred school, university or career. Fear of failure is embedded in the life experience of many people.

In their psychological study of university students and their parents, Elliot and Thrash argue that "by transferring fear of failure to their children, parents saddle their children with a dispositional burden that they must carry with them into each new achievement situation and that affects the goals they choose to pursue" (Elliot and Thrash 2004, 968). Carolyn Jackson (2003) argues that a fear of failure can lead directly to poor behavior and disengagement by young men in schools.

In "Creative" practices, however, failure is a necessary part of the creative process. It is embraced and explored rather than avoided (see Naray-Davey & Hurley, 2014). A "fail fast" approach is also typical among entrepreneurs, particularly in the US (Babineaux and Krumboltz 2013, Hall 2007). Here the mantra helps identify which products or services are likely to succeed in the long term and avoids wasting time. Similarly, digital fabrication practices are a useful way of "failing fast". A "draft" object can be printed for minimal cost (once the 3D printer itself has been purchased). Plastic filament is not expensive, so trial runs and adjustments are commonplace. Often, the physical act of printing demonstrates a "theoretical" problem with the digital version. 3D printing technology is also still developing, and it is not uncommon to encounter glitches or unexpected errors in the processes of translating data into things. Yet many of our project participants were visibly distressed and vocally expressed their disappointment when a print did not work perfectly the first time. Their responses were frequently framed along expressions of "trust me to get it wrong" or "of course it didn't work, I'm no use at it". As one of the facilitators who assisted our project indicated, "failure for us is not an option". The people in the "hard-to-reach" communities targeted by the project had already experienced so many difficulties in their lives that the facilitators did not want to engage them in a project only for them to experience another failure. Entrepreneurial philosophies did not work in this context.

"In the Making" was based in Salford, identified as one of the most deprived areas in the UK (Department for Communities and Local Government 2015). Mental and physical health conditions affect many residents, unemployment figures are high, criminal activity is common. People struggle for basic resources – accommodation, food, travel. For the "In the Making" project, the participants' status as disabled people compounded these existing challenges since "disabled people remain more likely to live in poverty, to have fewer educational qualifications, to be out of work and experience prejudice and abuse" (Cabinet Office, 2005). The project participants' self-perceptions were negatively affected by prevalent media narratives of disabled and unemployed people as burdens, a drain on public resources: "The period in 2010-11 saw more discussion of disability benefits in terms of being a claimed drain on the economy and a burden on the state [...] some articles even blaming the recession itself on incapacity benefit claimants" (Briant et al. 2011, 9).

In these community settings, a common phrase was: "I'm just not creative" echoing eighteenth-century poet William Blake's concept of the "mind forg'd manacles". Literary critic David Gross identifies such manacles or restraints for the mind as self-limiting thoughts, which are "a powerful cultural force" (1986. 3).[1]

These factors combine to present significant barriers to people considering themselves to be "creative" and to willingly access and engage with ostensibly creative activities. Yet when encouraged to participate and to understand their activities as their own productive experiences, we were able to engage initially uncertain people in a creative process. In the following section, I describe key steps that the facilitators took to democratize and foster creative activity. The project team sought to establish an atmosphere where creative failure was seen as a positive experience, however, those delivering the project also had an ethical imperative to avoid other kinds of failure at all costs. As "In the Making" developed a series of creative activities to develop 3D printing ideas, an experienced community arts practitioner said: "Disabled people have had a lifetime of damaging negativity. We have two days to build them up." The project needed to ensure that the community engagement and facilitation of activities were carefully worked through because negative experiences would add to a life-long narrative of limiting events. The next sections describe four key procedures which proved effective in supporting creative engagement and developing confidence in creative practice.

Ideas first, parameters next

3D printing is an exciting technology that is very good at gaining people's interest. However, a printer is only as good as the design it is programmed to produce. Experts from the digital fabrication community advise consistently that creative practice lies at the heart of unlocking the potential of 3D printing: "that idea of saying 'make whatever you want' is quite a frightening thing" (Armson 2015, n. pag.). Hence the first day of the two-day course was spent exploring ideas rather than engaging with the technology. In any context, too much choice can be overwhelming. To posit the question: "if you could make anything, what would you make?" is just as likely to shut down creative responses as it is to elicit imaginative triumphs. Inviting people to offer ideas can expose them to judgement and feelings of vulnerability. Too much choice can be overwhelming. The application of simple incremental procedures and parameters, in the manner of the Oulipo experimental literary

---

[1] The poem "London" by William Blake was written @ 1790: "In every cry of every Man, / In every Infants cry of fear, / In every voice: in every ban, / The mind-forg"d manacles I hear" Full text available at: http://www.poetryfoundation.org/poems-and-poets/poems/detail/43673

practice, proved effective in engaging a "ludic mode" for negotiating such barriers (Gallix 2013, n. pag.). Applying established modes of creative practice, in which various parameters or restrictions stimulate innovative responses is therefore likely to make the task more approachable. This is where strategies borrowed from innovative and experimental creative writing practice begin to bear fruit: "The Oulipo escapes the Romantic cul-de-sac of unfettered imagination (or its Surrealist avatar, chance) by reintroducing external constraints, which are self-imposed" (Ibid.). With a framework inviting step-by-step, simple responses, anxieties about being creative were assuaged as participants found that they achieved good ideas which surpassed their own expectations. These techniques will be unfolded in detail in a later section.

Purposeful meandering

"When are we going to do something?" asked an anxious participant after the first hour of the first morning appeared to have been spent in making tea, chatting, and fiddling about with the printers. In fact, this was deliberate time for participants to settle into the space, to begin building a group dynamic, and for the facilitators to understand the range and nature of the disabilities which required their support (participants were not required to disclose or categorize their conditions before attending, although they were invited to do so if they wished). This time also provided a "buffer" for late arrivals (common owing to health or travel difficulties), allowing them to join the space without drawing attention to themselves or disrupting an activity. The organic structure of the workshop, dictated in part by the diverse range of physical and mental abilities present, at first worried some of the facilitators, who feared that the session had degenerated into disparate activities, with some people doodling, others chatting, some wandering about or even taking a nap. However, offering people the opportunity to work at their own pace and in their own way, according to their need for rest or stimulation, was strongly welcomed by participants, who valued the informality and the fact that a strict timetable was not imposed. One participant e-mailed to say: "Today has inspired me to progress my deflated creativeness. Having a non-visual disability can't half get in the way and stop the things we aspire too [sic]... but todays [sic] atmosphere lifted me, everyones [sic] creative juices were flowing. The relaxed atmosphere and informative tuition was sublime... it helped me interact with people on all levels, sharing ideas and inspirations..." Announcing that "we are now going to create X" could have put people under pressure to achieve and might have been counter-productive in shutting down the unrestricted thinking upon which creative processes rely. Our project found that engaging participants in familiar activities which build gradually and organically into an emergent creative process can relieve such pressures.

Creative Failure, not "Failure to Create"

Meaningful creative practice is by nature experimental – original approaches may not work as intended and results can be unexpected. Becoming comfortable with failures is a necessary quality for the creative practitioner. However, project facilitators had an ethical responsibility not to fail their participants in delivering positive, creative experiences. Facilitators worked to become adept at delivering technical expertise while wearing their knowledge lightly. The vocabulary was discussed in advance to keep jargon to a minimum. The printers were given names and personalities so that if one developed a glitch, we could say that "Bob" was having a bad day, or that he didn't like the color of the filament he was printing. Facilitators developed what was almost a comedy routine in which banter and joking were encouraged. They would deliberately get things ridiculously wrong to show participants how easily it could be fixed. Trying to print a cup-holder 6 meters wide because the wrong scale had been employed in the software, for example. "There's always an 'undo' button," became a mantra for the trainers. Laughter dispels anxiety and encourages people to "have a go" because a precedent for creative failure has been established. If the "expert" gets it wrong, then it must be OK to mess up. While creative failure was built into the facilitation, a "failure to create" was avoided wherever possible. Sessions were designed to ensure that everyone made something and took home a unique 3D printed object, even if it was a simple keyring or a badge. The facilitators developed customizable templates so that someone with severe learning difficulties, for example, could still make choices about color and lettering.

Access to expert support

The availability of mentors and specialist knowledge can be a crucial factor in someone's development as a self-perceived creative individual. Offering advice and what would usually be hard-to-reach expensive guidance can encourage people to persevere with developing ideas, particularly when those ideas are validated by support from expert practitioners. Accordingly, individual support and mentoring proved to be one of the most effective drivers in empowering participants to explore their creativity. Appropriately skilled facilitators, who embody a skillset spanning creative and technical expertise, are scarce and costly. The project's budget was stretched in trying to secure the specialist support that we required. However, a half-hour chat with a product designer often generated unique ideas for assistive aids. The participant described his or her daily challenges and the product designer responded by framing a challenge as a design problem, co-constructing an idea for a product to meet that need. Guidance on how that design might progress technically could leave a participant motivated to work on developing their idea for the rest of the day, perhaps in part because an expert had told them that they had a "good idea". Some individuals felt empowered to continue working in their own time on the open-source software to which they had been introduced. The expert facilitator offered a bridge between lived experience, which is the raw material of an individual's creativity, and a response that is practically and perhaps commercially productive. An "expert" may also be seen as giving external validation to someone's idea, assuring them that their creativity is effective and their idea worth pursuing. Once someone had experienced the design process, they were able to continue independently. Some participants attended multiple courses with product ideas growing exponentially on each occasion. One participant said: "Ideas went off in my head and I realized that things are achievable. People will often say 'no' to what you want or need, but it opened my eyes to what can be created." An independent evaluation of participants' experiences can be found in Appendix 1.

Changing the story

Stories are powerful. They can shape identity, the self and how we relate to others. Charles Weingartner, reflecting once more upon William Blake's "mind forg'd manacles", asserts: "A shift in metaphors can produce a dramatic shift in the options and choices we perceive, conceive and then act on" (1997, 21). We noted earlier that disadvantaged and disenfranchised people are often the subject of negative portrayals in the mainstream media. Those who are unemployed and/or disabled tend to be portrayed as passive recipients of state support, and a drain on resources. A lifetime of exposure to such narratives is likely to damage self-esteem and thus, as we established earlier, inhibit individuals' ability to access their creativity. The first task of the inclusive FabLab is to shift the story away from the negative, to begin co-constructing new stories about empowerment, resourcefulness and participants being the authors of their own solutions. Throughout the workshops, people were encouraged to try things for themselves and to celebrate their own achievements rather than waiting for the experts to do it for them. To echo the ethos at FabLab Belfast, wherever it was safe and practical to do so, we "handed the hammer" to participants, even if this resulted in a lengthy and difficult process requiring a lot of the expert facilitator's input. The results in terms of confidence and self-esteem were worth a thousand-fold the resource deployed.

Play as a creative enabler

The first task for the inclusive FabLab is to create a safe and nurturing atmosphere in which perceptions of risk and failure are re-positioned as part of a playful process in which we can "mess about" without consequence. As Norman Jackson puts it, to "recognize emergent unanticipated outcomes" with calm curiosity rather than dismay at a plan going awry (Jackson 2003, 7). A communal, preliminary act of making tea and sharing biscuits, for example, helped create a group identity. Apparent small-talk, eliciting the stories of people's journeys to the venue, or their reasons for being there, initiated creative sharing and introduced storytelling as a core activity. "Guerilla creativity", where the intention or nature of the activity is not pre-announced, can be an effective way of getting around initial anxieties and preconceptions. This may continue with activities involving elements of meditation, visualization and relaxation. The effects of such activities are intended to shift the group dynamic into a more creative and receptive state, engaging imagination, daydreaming, and transcending the constraints of the everyday.

To function effectively in a late capitalist society, we are schooled to be logical, rational and reasonable. We have routines, appointments, schedules and reminders. We write lists and complete tasks in a linear fashion. To engage with state services such as health and welfare, such behaviors are expected and necessary if support is to be accessed successfully. A welfare service would understandably take a dim view of someone who was late for an appointment because they had a great idea and stopped to think about it. Therefore, most of us find our rational, critical faculties to be strongly developed, perhaps to the point where they allow the speculative and the imaginative little room to exist. "Society has overvalued rationality and technology at the expense of losing from consciousness a fundamental sense of 'authentic being'..." (Childers and Hentzi 1995, 103). This overvaluing of rationality in fact does not serve the knowledge economy, where lateral thinkers and radical innovators are future wealth generators. Indeed, this pressure to get things right "can result in a risk-averse attitude that does not allow for exploration and discovery" (Naray-Davey and Hurley 2014, 6).

Creating a space in which people are freed, temporarily, from the constraints of conventional logic, reason and sense, is therefore necessary if new ideas and imaginative responses are to be accessed: "openness to experience had the largest effect [on developing creativity]: as openness increased, people were much more likely to be doing something creative" (Silvia et al. 2014, 185). The means to creating that openness, we found, are to lower the stakes by encouraging provisionality, play and peer support to try things out. "Just having a play" became a phrase in the 3D printing workshops that allowed participants to experiment without the pressure to succeed with a tangible outcome. This resonates with Baker's findings on "serious play" and her critique of the "western positivist view of play, which sees play as trivial" (Baker 2004,199). Baker uses Schechner's (1994) work on performance to reconfigure play as "serious, real and privileged – 'the divine process of creating'" (Baker 2004,199).

The strategies unfolded here became the underlying principles of our inclusive FabLab, whereby demystification, "bitesize" incremental activities, simple choices, ludic modes and attention to usually unconscious processes widen access to our common creativity.

From idea to print

Nurturing people's creativity was our starting point in the inclusive FabLab. However, our collaborators needed effective processes to generate designs amenable to materialization. The translation of an idea to a printable prototype was the most complex aspect of the workshop process, and the point at which we had to be most watchful to safeguard our participants from negative experiences of failure. The following fieldnotes from an early workshop illustrate the practical and conceptual challenges.

> *Immediate thoughts/responses following Day 1 of Workshop 1*
>
> *Present: the three research leads, an arts facilitator; a FabLab expert and a community support volunteer attended the afternoon session.*
>
> *Participants: two profoundly autistic young people, accompanied by their social worker;*
>
> *a young woman receiving arts on prescription for a mental health condition, supported by her father; an older woman, medically retired, using a large electric wheelchair, supported by a paid assistant. All present had lived experience of disability, either as supporters/family or primary experiencer.*
>
> *General outcome: Despite setbacks with the facilitation, participants seemed to enjoy the activities and to engage enthusiastically.*
>
> *Reflective response: I was relieved about this but also disappointed that we didn't get better value out of our facilitators. The interface between arts practice and technology seems to be a gulf that we couldn't get around.*
>
> *Observations/insights:*
>
> *Participants had not received the advance e-mail containing the artist facilitator's preparatory tasks, even though I sent this twice to one of our volunteers for distribution. Learning point – in future, consider critical points of failure and ensure that professional researchers retain ownership. Check that facilitators are comfortable working in unpredictable environments.*

The artist did manage to improvise a task, but this delayed progress into actual making. Sharing a good thing and bad thing that happened to everyone in the past week was a useful way in to the ideas process. The group dynamic seemed friendly and supportive. The young woman attending with arts on prescription did not wish to answer this task but was drawn into further conversations and was proactively initiating conversations by the end of the day. A notable, positive change here. She became outgoing and chatty. The wheelchair user spoke a lot about access and travel. She gave a repeated account of attending a family event, involving a long journey and a hotel room inaccessible due to clutter.

Several people said: "I'm just not creative."

Introducing objects from bags/pockets worked well.

Participants enjoyed the concept of "using imagination to turn anything into anything". They liked the idea of sending a birthday present to someone as a 3D file that the recipient could print.

Every participant shared a personally significant and effectively shaped narrative. One of the autistic participants spoke movingly about the two small red leaves in the wallet of her travel card. She noticed them on the ground outside an event and couldn't work out where they had come from. She thought them symbolic. She was prompted to consider symbolic of what? Two = significant. "The leaves show that there are people like you when you don't think there are people like you."

The participant using a wheelchair was very interested in assistive aids. Her key turning device seemed highly significant. "It would be nice to make one in a jazzy color. My front door is my haven and my home."

The father of the young woman receiving arts on prescription was also concerned with keys. He had two sets of car keys with him, one spare set which he always carries following difficulties with lost or locked-in keys in his past. We talked about the car representing freedom/independence. He was keen at lunchtime to drive home for dinner and considered returning his laptops to the car or taking them home, so the possibility of travel, particularly to return to home as a haven for physical nourishment and security seemed uppermost in his mind.

A more general discussion about the technology involved one charity worker confiding that his colleagues were very cynical about FabLabs and questioned why their organization should be involved but now they are sending him links about 3D printing, "like their imaginations are being fired up".

One participant commented about being "awestruck by the compassionate nature" of what could be achieved by digital fabrication, e.g. printing prosthetic limbs for children.

The artist facilitator noted "beautifully crafted stories from people who claim not to be creative".

We moved from conversation into working with clay. One participant had difficulty with this due to manual strength/dexterity, but the arts facilitator and the participant's care worker helped, and she progressed to writing. Key words for her were: "disability", "finance" and then "flowers". There seemed to be a progression from practical worries and barriers into a more imaginative and aesthetic space. She had the idea of making a cuff out of flowers/letters. As figure 3.3 shows, the artist facilitator noted the lovely flow of the handwriting and tasked our technical facilitators with finding a way to capture this in a 3D print. Eventually they succeeded (see Chapter 4).

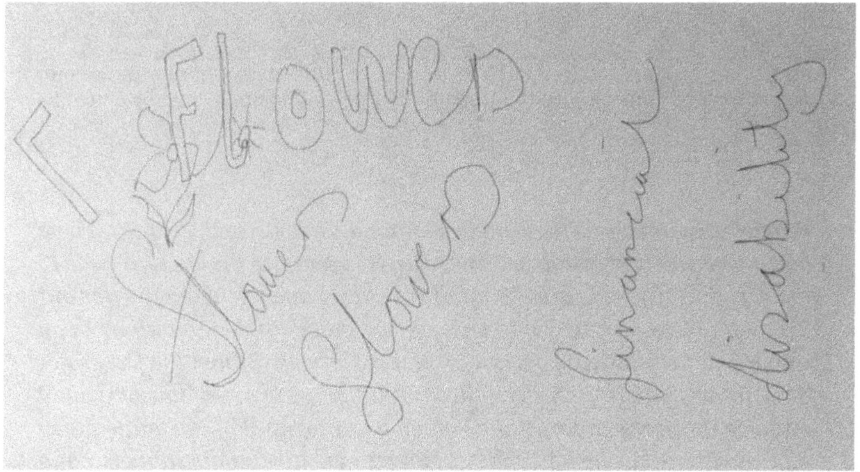

Figure 3.3. A participant's initial notes for an idea to print.

Given the technical complexity, I searched for a pre-existing file on Thingiverse that we could adapt but couldn't find anything. My own lack of knowledge is frustrating.

The clay produced lots of engaged making, with imaginative textures and shapes being created, as shown in Figure 3.4.

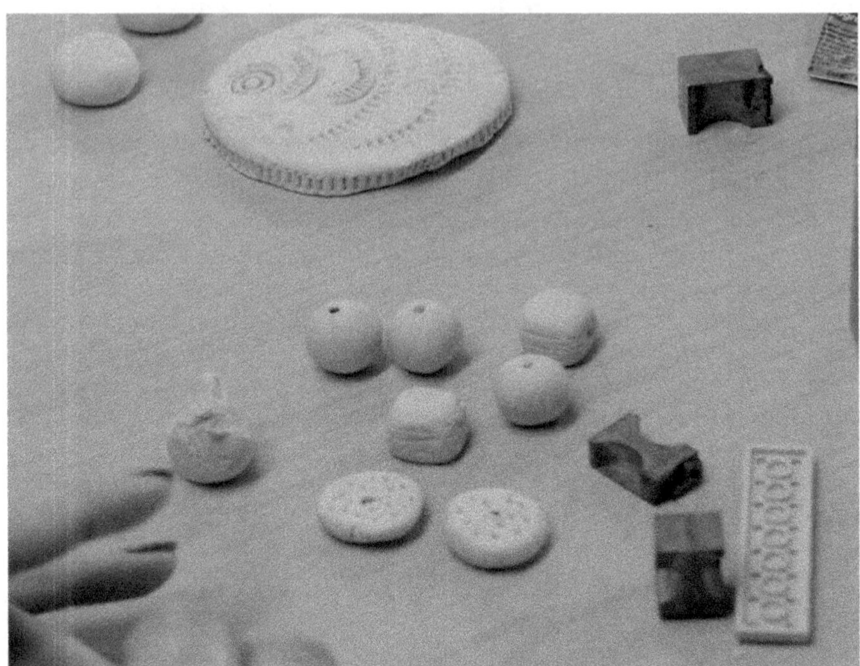

Figure 3.4. Participants engaged enthusiastically with the invitation to experiment with shape and texture, moving into the three-dimensional thinking needed to create a 3D print.

People talked freely as they made. Humor and repartee developed. There was a discussion of collaborative creativity. However, the obvious issue to me was that the scale and detail of the clay shapes were too fine for our 3D scanners to pick up and hence we would be unable to import them into the design software. Despite a preparatory workshop, the facilitator does not seem alert to the technical limitations. I worried how we would manage this foreseeable failure, which was the result of the fault-line in our facilitation being split between creative practitioners and technically adept individuals.

Mindful of participants' comfort and energy levels, we had planned frequent breaks and a long, early lunch. However, the lunch break was perhaps too soon and too long? It broke the group dynamic, which never returned. One autistic participant disengaged completely and crouched by the radiator for the rest of the day, making occasional comments to question or contradict facilitators.

Happily, the other autistic participant was highly engaged with the printers throughout and was soon operating the manual dial, selecting demo prints.

The head of the venue hosting us came in at lunch and we talked with her about the possibilities. Everyone agreed on the need to move beyond the clever gimmick to find out how people can really use the technology.

When the expert arrived from FabLab the tables were covered in craft. The artist facilitator had just started moving people to thinking about bead shapes and making. One of our participants correctly pointed out that they would be too small to scan – see figure 3.5. There was some engagement with the beads, but we never moved into putting them together into a piece. There was too little time before the FabLab facilitator arrived (his input makes more sense at the end of day 2). Even he doesn't understand the 3D scanners, so they appear to be an expensive waste of resource.

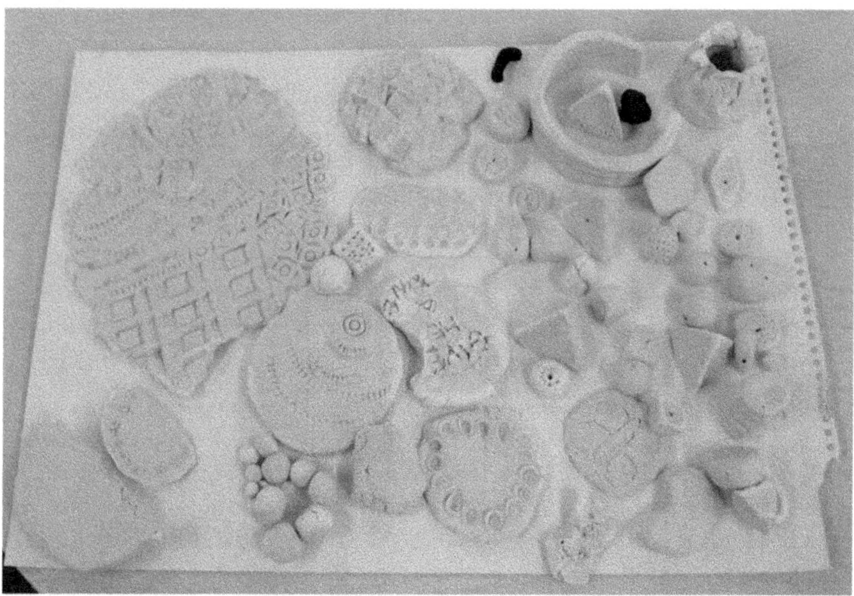

Figure 3.5. Despite a productive session with the clay shapes, the detail was too fine for the 3D scanners to capture – ultimately these shapes did not progress into digitally fabricated objects. However, the activity did help to establish the social benefits of communal making activities and helped us to finetune the approach for the next workshop.

Once the tech expert began talking the making stopped. He was very engaging, and people chipped in and asked questions, but it deadened the creative space. It was a mistake to ask him to explain FabLabs – I suggested he explain them because several participants had never heard of a FabLab and asked repeatedly what it was, so I saw this as awareness raising and bridging to further practice. This echoes the question raised by the Falmouth FabLab visit – "is the purpose to produce a breakthrough design and product, or to raise awareness through show and tell?". In fact, the young woman referred to us via arts on prescription was very interested in accessing laser cutters and the associated costs, so it was useful for her.

The session became a round-table discussion with the social worker expressing strong opinions about the need for a creative space to develop ideas away from FabLab. People don't learn by going to the open sessions because someone does it for them. Confirming the findings of our site visits, there was repeated reference to a lack of human resources in FabLabs, juggling time and attention between users with diverse needs. Extra funding could allow them to open for community benefit 7 days a week. This would, however, require a significant investment/resource.

I grew increasingly uncomfortable with the direction of the day, aware of too much talking and not enough making. Eventually, I intervened to bring us back to scanning. We managed a demo with a hacked piece of kit based on an Xbox Kinect, which the FabLab expert had brought with him – some participants visibly enjoyed this process, with one scanning another, the results of which can be seen in Figures 3.6 and 3.7. At my prompting, the tech expert explained how this could become a 3D file and be exported to print. Some of the group were very interested. But how do we move beyond 3D selfies?

It became apparent that time and funding for creative and technical facilitators to work together to better understand each other's practice was necessary before the sessions with participants. One person with both a craft and a technical skillset would be ideal, but our project has been unable to locate anyone within the geographical area. There is a gulf that needs bridging. Briefing is an issue: I hadn't been able to discuss the session with the technical facilitator in person and he came back from leave to instructions left by someone who had gone on leave. Staffing and resource issues mean that frequently we don't know until the day of the workshop who FabLab are able to send, or even if they can spare anyone at all.

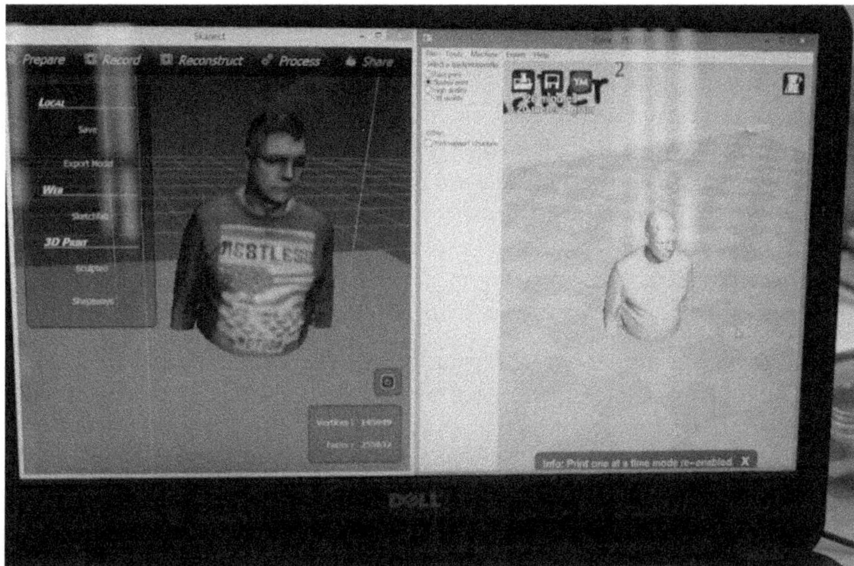

Figure 3.6. The scanner image (left) being converted to a format compatible with the printer (right).

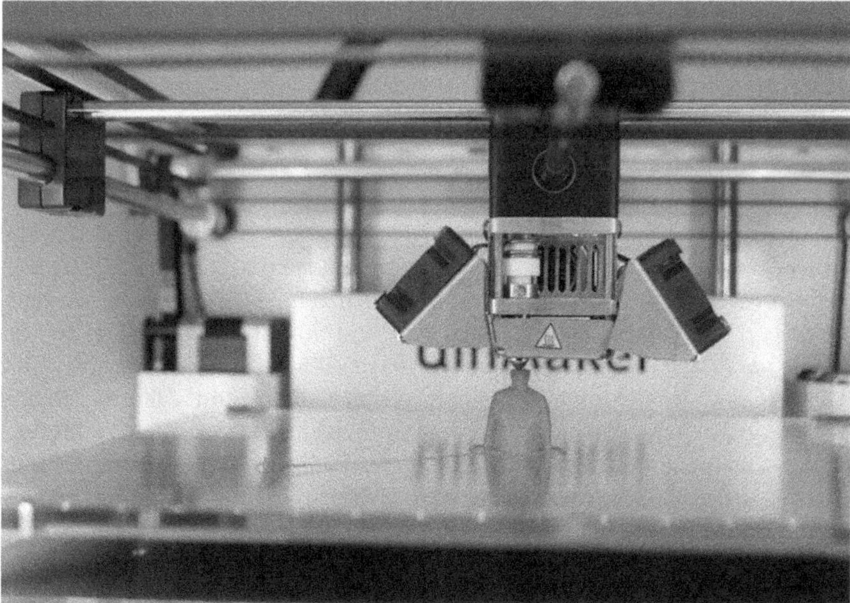

Figure 3.7. The 3D selfie emerging from the printhead. Many participants, particularly those on the autistic spectrum, found this process highly engaging.

The arts facilitator expressed strong and interesting views on the interactions. She felt it was political – the politics of disability. She was shocked at how people were defining themselves as "autistic" (one participant wore a laser-cut pendant of the word around her neck), or the way in which the wheelchair user-defined herself by disability and financial implications. We reflected on what appeared to be self-limiting narratives imposed through the internalizing of dominant discourses. We agreed that a danger throughout the project is of looking only at practical needs, not attending to the creative, aesthetic, and spiritual needs of a whole person. We need further conversation to unpack this.

As scanning went on, the group dynamic broke down, with a community volunteer getting up to make tea and interrupting other interactions to ask everyone what they wanted. The artist had to leave promptly, as did the social worker but everyone else was happy to stay and chat and ask more about the technology.

Field notes, Salford, September 2015

This reflective account of an early workshop captures the great potential of digital fabrication, not only to engage people's imaginations and bring them into social making spaces, but also the unique things that disabled people could design and make, with the right support and resources. What this account also captures, however, is the difficulty of creating an effective inclusive FabLab, where the facilitation empowers people to generate original ideas that are achievable prototypes with the time, equipment and expertise available.

As the workshop account attests, the hinge of complexity within the process of digital fabrication is in distilling an idea and then expressing it in a form intelligible to computer-controlled machines. This is the interface between creative and technical skill sets, and the most demanding step for participants in the inclusive makerspace. While evolving an inclusive FabLab practice, we were subject to false steps and failures. Digital fabrication depends on a mix of creative and technical skills. The facilitators and researchers frequently encountered knowledge gaps and mistranslations across disciplines as we worked to develop a mobile, inclusive making space. I am a novice 3D printer, and this helped to frame the activities from the perspective of the participants, rather than the experts. However, some of the creative facilitators found the technology and its current limitations highly frustrating, while the technical experts struggled to explain things in lay-person's terms. While we did provide a training day for the creative facilitators, a key learning point from the project is that much more time and resource need devoting to creative and technical experts working together, to learn each other's languages and to explore how they might collaborate more effectively. The great responsibility was to manage those failures carefully so as not to fail our co-constructors, who were already all too familiar with experiences of rejection, difficulty and obstruction. While "creative failure" is to be expected (indeed invited as part of the creative process), a failure to create required careful management for our collaborators, who may have perceived the experience as reinforcing lifelong narratives of inadequacy and lack. Our aim, therefore, was that every participant should leave with a 3D printed object that was unique and personally meaningful.

Poetry as a process

The project explored different facilitation strategies to elicit and evolve ideas for things to print, including routines drawn from experimental poetic practices. These routines are set out in detail by Hazel Smith (2005) in *The Writing Experiment: Strategies for Innovative Creative Writing*. While the role of poetry in our inclusive maker space may seem tenuous, perhaps even exclusive, Titchkosky (2011) finds "poetic knowledge" and "disability" in the same place, "emerging in the intersection of the perceiver and the perceived" to question "how we make the meaning of people" (131). Lucas Introna (2014) adds material possibilities to the argument: "The 'poetic' is taken here not in the sense of a romantic nostalgia but rather in the sense of a bringing forth that allows things to disclose themselves in their own terms" (52). Combined with digital fabrication, the practice also allows people to disclose themselves in their own terms, through the embodiment of the imagination, troubling the ways in which disability is "cast as a strict matter of the body" (Titchkosky 2011, 131).

With these possibilities in mind, we designed the creative facilitation to explore the poetic potential of making. Here is one of the creative exercises devised by arthur+martha CIC:

Bound about with dreams

This is a project to make a bracelet or cuff, worn as a reminder to follow your own path. The starting point for the bracelet might be made of objects, textures, words, that mean something to you. We will design on paper or in 3D, then continue on computer and finally print your ideas as a wearable 3-dimensional sculpture.

The making will come out of discussions about what makes you feel free and what traps you. The questions below are a start point for conversations about this - and to get the making started.

You'll need to bring some small objects with you and some ideas. Below we've suggested a few objects and there are also some questions for you to think about. Try to answer them in 9 words.

Qs

What represents freedom to you - and why?

When or where do you feel trapped?

Where do you go to in your imagination?

Describe the most beautiful piece of jewelry ever seen...

Objects

Bring a selection of objects that fit in your hand - things that mean a lot to you. They might be happy associations, or important in another way.

Bring a bag of small, nicely shaped objects. Things that FEEL good to you.

Bring a letter or message that you want to remember, it could be an email or text. Preferably bring the original letter so that it can be scanned.

***

While scanning objects proved less productive within the limitations of our equipment, the simple questions routine was pleasingly fruitful. Progressing from process to product, one route to printing was to use text itself as a direct source of material. As will be illustrated shortly, our technical facilitators developed a process for printing 3D text, which could be purposed as wearable (a badge or a cuff), or as a wall-plaque, paperweight, or ruler. From the poetic material, participants selected text, typed or dictated the words into the software, made aesthetic decisions about design, color and font, and then wore their own words in a fascinating performance of embodied auto/biography.

Figures 3.8 – 3.14 represent the diversity of responses:

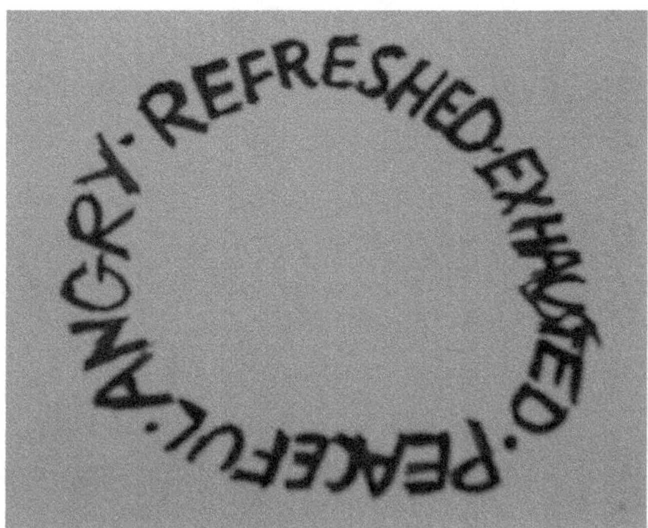

Figure 3.8. The content and the typography combine to express strongly contrasting physical states and accompanying emotions. Our facilitators worked to find ways of preserving the unique handwritten quality of these texts.

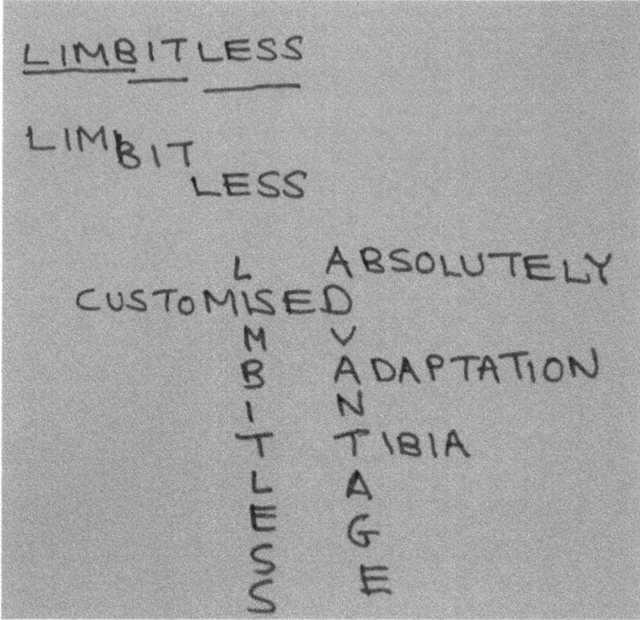

Figure 3.9. This participant chose to play with language to express possibilities presented by digital fabrication, producing a pun on "limb" and "limit" in this crossword design.

Figure 3.10. This maker chose to express contrasts through physical and mental embodied states. Again, the calligraphy is distinctive. We looked to develop methods of preserving flourishes and embellishments in the final print.

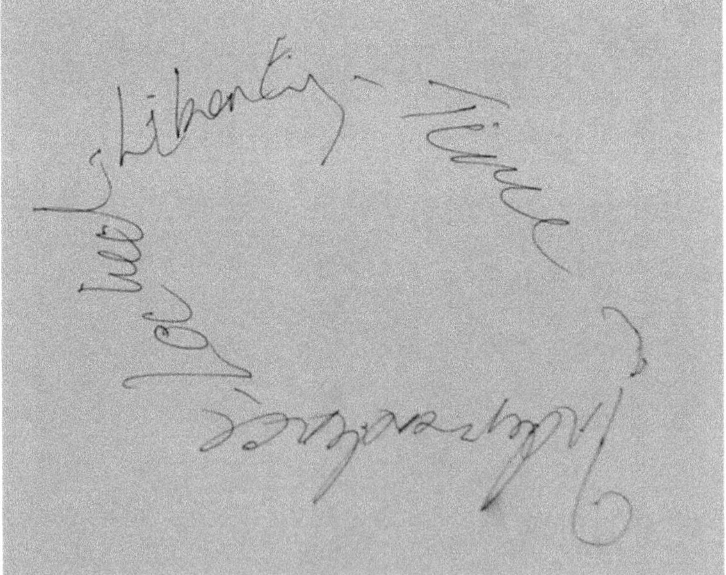

Figure 3.11. This maker's physical condition caused difficulty in writing, but also produced a beautiful, flowing script, which our artist facilitator felt had great potential aesthetically.

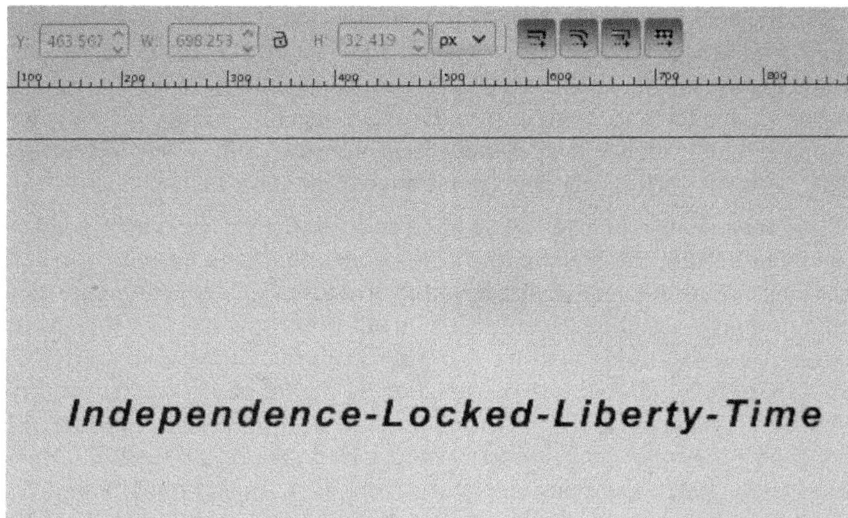

Figure 3.12. Our technical facilitators developed a simple method for typing text into Inkscape (freely available open-source software). Inkscape allows variation in typeface, size and effects such as bold or italic. Most participants were able to select and enter their text themselves. Facilitators then exported the file to the 3D printer software, which was able to read the text as relief or embossed lettering.

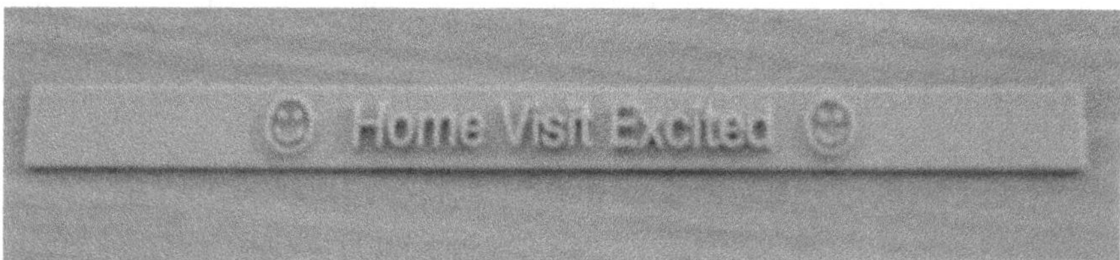

Figure 3.13. Text and simple graphics produced via the Inkscape technique. Participants selected words, emojis, and the color of the print filament.

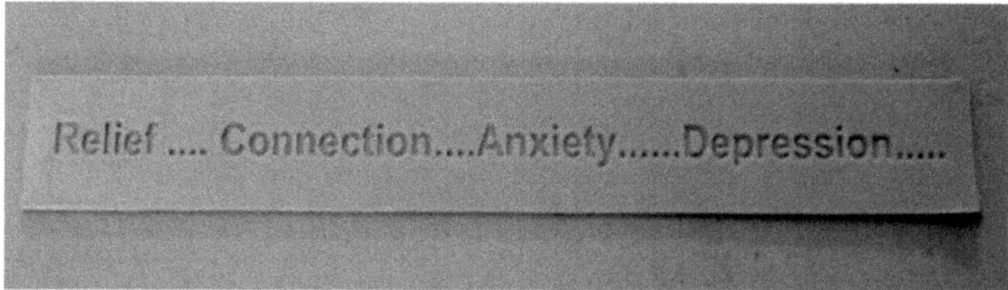

Figure 3.14. This maker chose to depress the text to echo the experience of depression. They chose to use this print as a ruler, but if submerged in hot water, the PLA filament used by our printers could be bent to form a wearable cuff. Facilitators worked very carefully with participants who chose to make a cuff, ensuring that the water was not too hot, nor the cuff too tight.

The project's technical and creative facilitators soon became adept at using these simple poetic procedures to generate personally meaningful wearable text with our participants. People appeared pleased and enthusiastic about the text-objects that they had created, showing them eagerly to friends, family and supporters to evidence their successful engagement with a new technology. There seem to be clear wins here for self-esteem and social interaction.

The very short forms of these wearable texts may also carry political potential beyond the literal content. For some, the required brevity of text selected for printing opened a creative space. Such modes of expression circumvent the traditional requirement in auto/biography for "a self-identical coherence across time and space that was capable of narration" (Barrett 2014, 1571). Carefully selected text can function as the tip of an iceberg, carrying depths of experience and association beneath it, without needing the connective tissue of how and why. Donna Haraway in her seminal *Cyborg Manifesto* (1991) identifies miniaturization as a potent and potentially dangerous ideological activity: "Miniaturization has turned out to be about power; small is not so much beautiful as pre-eminently dangerous…" (153). In the case of miniaturized narratives, what kind of power might be involved? In what ways might they be dangerous, and to whom? Our project suggests that disabled makers harnessed 3D printing technology to produce subversive concrete texts which challenge and disrupt hegemonic constructs of disabled people as objects of pity and lack.

How do they do this? Minimalist texts ask a lot of their readers. In the examples above, the reader senses expansive emotional landscapes and physical events beneath the few words chosen to materialize as a print. Generated via poetic concentration and selection, such texts present a snapshot, weighted with backstory from which readers might construct the potential experiences of the disabled author. They pose an invitation for the reader to imagine their way into the embodied reality of the maker, prompting the reader to wonder "what is it like to be you?", and perhaps achieving a more compassionate understanding of disabling circumstances as a result. Formally, such minimalist texts hint at complex and difficult life stories, but in their brevity, they offer no closure, indeed there is no definitive ending. Haraway might see this as a political action, extrapolating the refusal of closure as a refusal of the ultimately Oedipal narratives of the Western canon. A text which does not depend upon the plot of original unity could signal the literature of a post-human world, a world which is less hierarchical, and which is more open to differently-abled ways of being (1991, 150).

Whereas longer narrative forms must go to a great deal of effort to create and then explain their attempt to refuse closure, miniature narratives by their very nature present polymorphous versions of themselves, creating "pleasure in the confusion of boundaries" (Haraway 1991, 176). Encountering "the play of a text that has no finally privileged reading" (ibid.) demands imaginative and intellectual engagement; the encounter does not allow passivity. Readers are not consumers but co-creators alongside the author, de-hierarchizing traditional reader/writer dynamics, and perhaps the boundaries of self and "other".

Rather than spending hours interfacing with a text, in the way that a traditional narrative is consumed, the physical interface with a miniature narrative is very brief. It may take moments to read the text, but that text is then saved to the reader's own memory where, like a computer program, it begins to run. In its interaction with the reader's unique imaginative and contextual circumstances, such a miniaturized narrative might live on for hours, days, maybe years, as something which no longer exists as a physical interaction, but in the memory circuits of readers who in a sense come to embody the text. What we can see here is the "powerful infidel heteroglossia" (Haraway 1991, 181) of the cyborg text which Haraway imagines as an experimental "'ethnography'" (1991, 162). Not so much written on the body as in it, writing and re-writing itself within the neural pathways of the living reader. Texts made by hand with pipe-cleaners, for example (shown later in this book), and then imported into a 3D printer speak particularly strongly to this embodied quality, a transmission of lived experience, via concrete text, from one human being to another. The fact that one can hold the text at the same time as reading it melds physical and intellectual processes in intriguing ways. A 3D printed version of the text privileges its presence so that it demands sensory attention, giving it a material status, which may make such miniaturized and concretized narratives particularly suited to asserting the testimony of marginalized people documenting their own experiences.

Miniature narratives can be so weighted with symbolism, or have such an apparent lack of plot, that they may cross into the territory of prose poems (resonating our poetic methodology). Miniature narratives question and problematize and worry at generic boundaries. The confusion in naming and defining such texts adds to their refusal of categorization, eclectic nature, and kaleidoscopic incarnations. By their very natures miniature narratives push genre to breaking point – when does a narrative cease and a collection of words emerge? To use the analogy of a black hole, perhaps the material contained within miniature narrative has become condensed to the point where it is beginning to collapse upon itself, until it creates a rift in the reality of text as we know it, where the rules of genre do not apply. Haraway does not make the link explicitly, but I believe that miniature narrative is one of the arenas in which "our story-tellers [are] exploring what it means to be embodied in high-tech worlds" (Haraway 1991, 173). In this case, it is disabled people who are taking the role of story-tellers and intersecting the complex experiences of disability with the material potential of digital fabrication to explore and articulate post-anthropocentric embodiment.

Miniature narratives threaten the realist narrative, indeed challenge established concepts of "reality" as they celebrate the transfer of creative power, explode genre and make themselves at home in our polymorphous Ethernet culture, as they, like 3D designs, become virtual, viral, collective, distributed endlessly in digital form. Subverting post-modern nihilism and ennui, miniature narratives are proving wrong the theorists who claim there is nothing to be done but imitate. Frederic Jameson, for example, claims that "in a world in which stylistic innovation is no longer possible, all that is left is to imitate dead styles, to speak through the masks and with the voices of the styles in the imaginary museum" (1998, 7). Our disabled makers may beg to differ. We may be witnessing the evolution of a post-postmodern form, capable of functioning in the post-anthropocentric era.

Collective/political making

Alongside individual articulations of experience, our project also tried to develop collective and communal poetic activity, in keeping with our interest in political making. Therefore, participants were invited to gather around a table, adding their responses in turn to a set of simple questions. Facilitator Philip Davenport, co-director of community arts group arthur+martha CIC, initiated collective poetry by posing questions and recording the responses of everyone around the table. Where necessary, this question was translated by interpreters. If anyone chose not to reply, this was respected as a valid response and the silence was recorded as a space on the page. So, in response to the questions "what makes you feel free?" and "what makes you feel trapped?" the following was recorded, with Davenport writing down the responses as they were spoken or translated:

trapped dyslexia
non-conformity free
independence
ditto
liberty
freedom captures and bounds us
no responsibility
being on outside
gravity
writing I can go wherever I like
flying much easier if I had wings
freedom of choice

driving
to be able to the shops
pressure – gotta do that, gotta do this
good health opens the doors
motorbikes
to see the horizon and climb higher
not having to justify

(Workshop notes, 16 September 2015)

When this collective text was read back to the group, its co-authors were able to recognize it as having literary merit, taking pleasure and satisfaction in hearing and reviewing their creation. The complex and double-edged assertion that freedom itself (or perhaps the idea of it) can capture and bind us has, in my opinion, strong poetic quality in that it can sustain multiple interpretive possibilities.

Interestingly, given the project's hunch about the possibilities of political making, the collective poem uses poetic knowledge to address a long-standing tension between individual accounts of life experiences and disability. Timothy Barrett, for instance, describes "intense antipathy and distrust within disability studies towards 'individualism'" (2014, 1571) and goes on to identify the logic that "auto/biographical life writing tends towards a consideration of disability primarily in terms of individual experience, perpetuating the psychologized tropes of tragedy, struggle and overcoming rather than patterns of structural oppression" (Ibid.). As was established in earlier discussion, dominant social narratives set an unfortunate precedent, implying that "ordinary" disabled people are simply not trying hard enough to live up to these inspiring examples, and draw attention away from the important work of identifying and critiquing the disabling social structures that underpin such positionings.

Our project's inclusive and collective creative procedures may offer one way of co-constructing accounts of lived experience which accommodate individual expression but also highlight the disabling factors of the social context in which the co-writers are located. The political potential of what people made in our project will be explored in detail in Chapter 4. Here it is enough to note that evident in the collective poem reproduced above is a sustained attention to physical positioning: going out, being outside, transitioning from one place to another via doors, or driving. Such a concern with "the way people are already situated" (Titchkosky 2011, 130) suggests a collective attention to independence and freedom of choice: hard-won, contested, and not to be taken for granted. Allusions to pressure and resistance to self-justification may speak to experiences of health and welfare systems whose requirements are becoming increasingly stringent in this period of austerity. For instance, the 2016 inquiry by the United Nations Committee on the Rights of Disabled Persons highlighted that benefits reforms in the UK "hindered disabled people's right to live independently and be included in the community" (BBC News 2016). In our project's collaborative poem, we may also find an implied critique of the medical model of health, where someone feels trapped by the fact of their dyslexia, resulting in a state of being which affects interior and exterior life. Indeed, many of the texts generated by our participants are notable for their attention to internal and external embodied experiences.

Thus, before we reach the stage of generating material interpretable to a 3D printer, the creative process itself does reflexive work, "constructing the poet himself or herself, even as the experience is unfolding. It is a self-revealing, self-constructing form of discovery" (Brady 2004, 630). Through this poetic routine, our collaborators explored and asserted self-hood – collectively and individually – while simultaneously developing techniques for articulating and ultimately materializing certain aspects of that self-hood via 3D printed objects. Detailed case studies of the outputs of these facilitation strategies will be presented in Chapter 4.

While poetry proved to be a surprisingly inclusive and effective methodology for generating original 3D prints, it did not suit everyone, and we were keen to offer as diverse a range of creative processes as possible. To this end, "In the Making" collaborated with another local project to share different approaches to creative facilitation. During her Research Fellowship on the AHRC Connected Communities project "Cultural Intermediation", Jessica Symons worked as an anthropologist with local people in a "hard-to-reach" area of Salford. During fieldwork, Symons found resistance to traditional representations of creative and cultural activities as constituting "art, music, theatre". Instead, people defined their own creative and cultural activity as spending time with friends and family and engaging with local events and interests. Building on insights gathered from ethnographic engagement and local intermediaries, Symons developed a new approach, called *Ideas4Ordsall*, which emphasized supporting local people to realize their own ideas for creative and cultural activities. The combination of local intermediary support and individual ownership of the ideas themselves resulted in a flourishing of community engagement. People were excited by the freedom that came with identifying their own areas of creative activity, developing their own ideas and working with people they already knew. Full details of the project may be found at: http://www.ideas4ordsall.org

Engaging in cross-project collaboration, we adapted one of Symons' strategies to generate personal avatars that "In the Making" participants could 3D print. The exercise was conducted in pairs, with support from a facilitator where appropriate. The approach is summarized here (with thanks to Jessica Symons):

Designing your own character

Step 1: Fill in the grid

	Creature	Why?
If you could be any animal what would it be?		
If you could be any bird what would it be?		
If you could be any sea creature what would it be?		
If you could be any fantasy figure what would it be?		

Step 2: Develop a character idea which combines the "why?" reasons in the table above. For example, if you like dogs because they are furry, robins because they are chirpy, sharks because they are dangerous and mermaids because they are swishy then create a character which is furry, chirpy, dangerous and swishy!

Making your character

Step 3: Get a blank piece of paper and, using the art materials available, create a character based on your character idea developed in Step 1 and 2.

Step 4: Show your character to the 3D printing expert to discuss how it can be finalized into a model to be printed using the 3D machines.

Step 5: Look at the different characters in your group and discuss what adventure they might have together. What journey would they like to go on? Where? Why? How? When? What for?

***

This exercise worked effectively and enjoyably for many participants who appeared to relish the combination of individual task and collective endeavor. Some of the outputs from this exercise are reproduced below in figures 3.15-3.19:

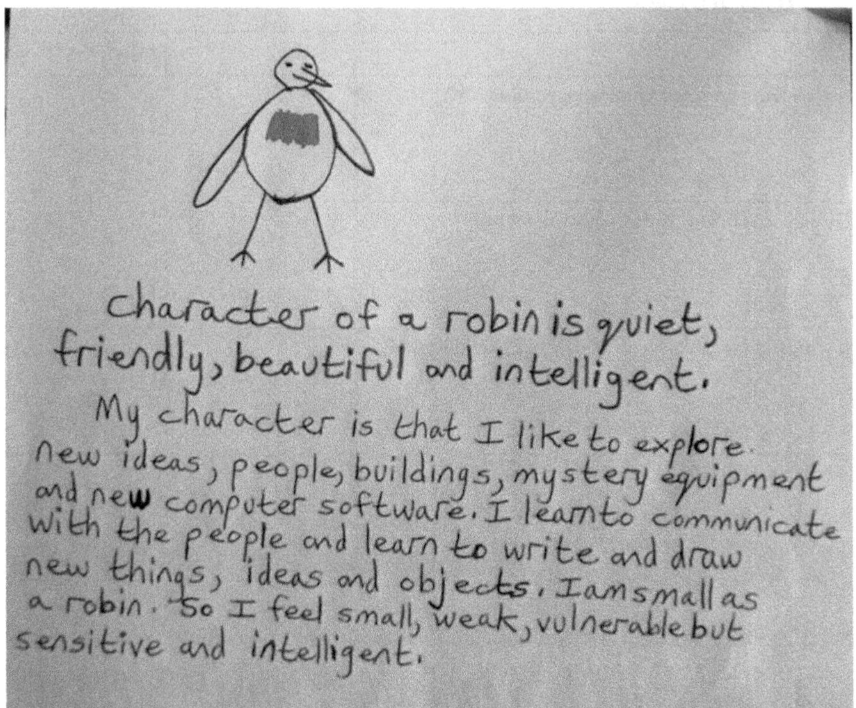

Figure 3.15. One participant's idea for a "robin" avatar, which reflects some of his experience of the workshop, as well as his embodiment as a disabled person.

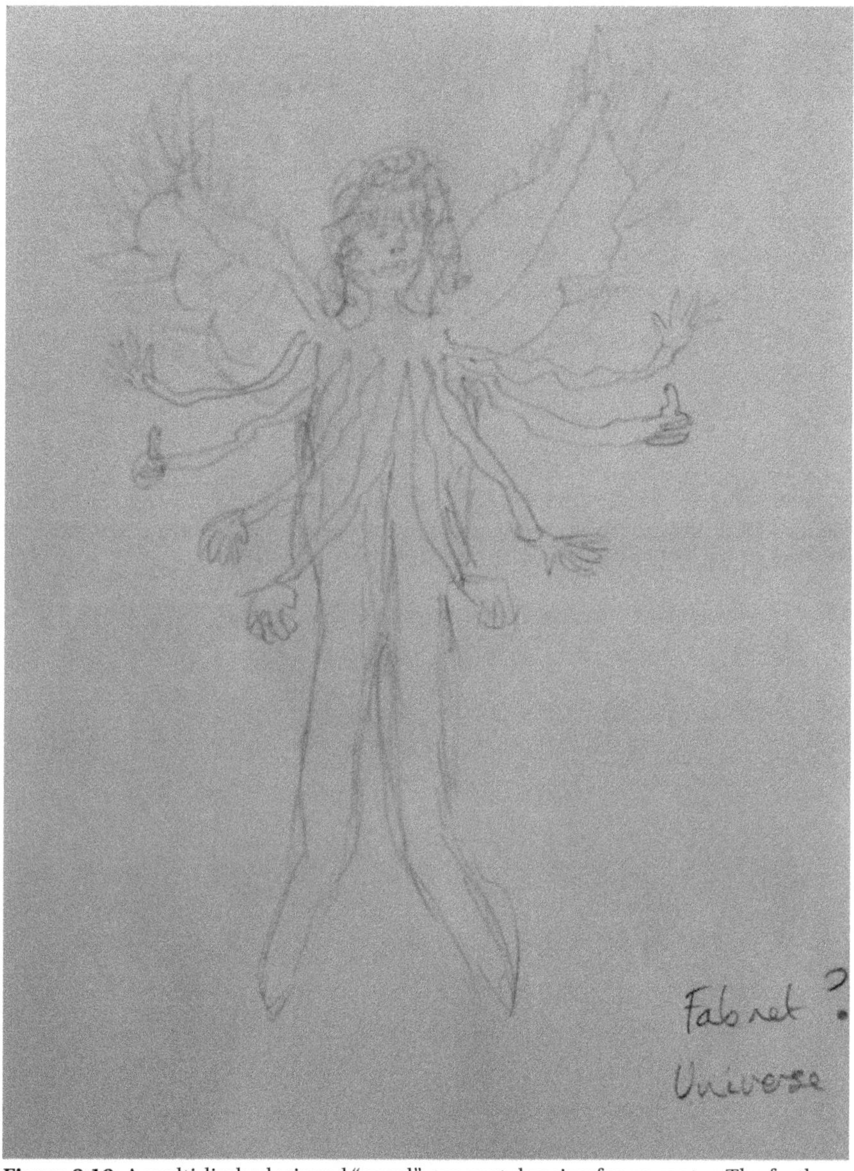

Figure 3.16. A multi-limbed winged "angel" concept drawing for an avatar. The feathers, hair and hands proved challenging to realize on our equipment.

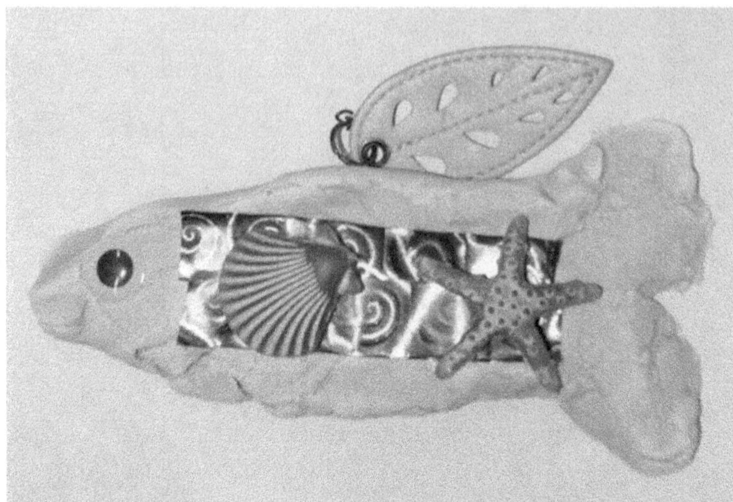

Figure 3.17. A tropical fish avatar, representing the maker's fluid identity and movement between ethnic and social statuses, on its way to being materialized.

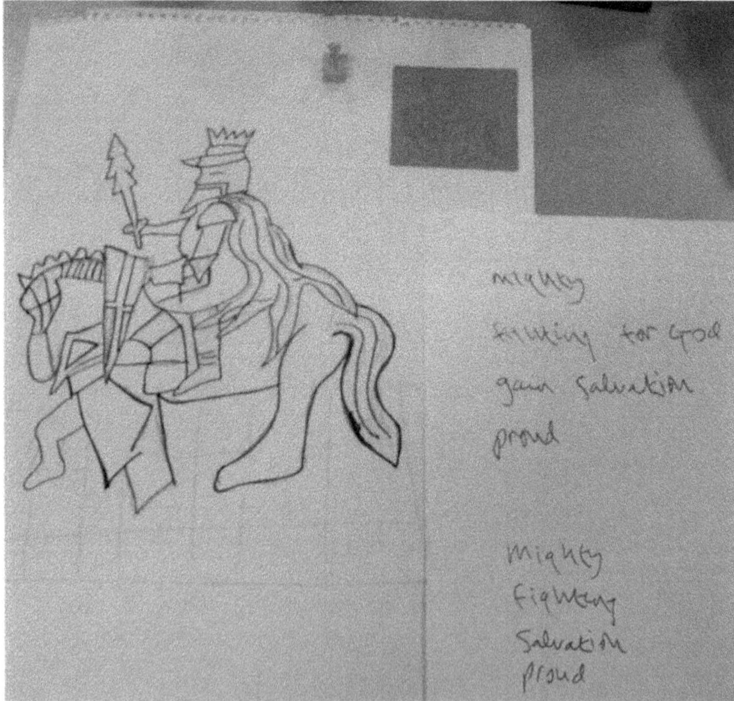

Figure 3.18. Initial text and scale drawing for a "mighty knight" avatar, representing for its maker strength, pride and salvation. A 3D printed chess figure, and a relief print of the scanned drawing are just visible in the top right-hand corner.

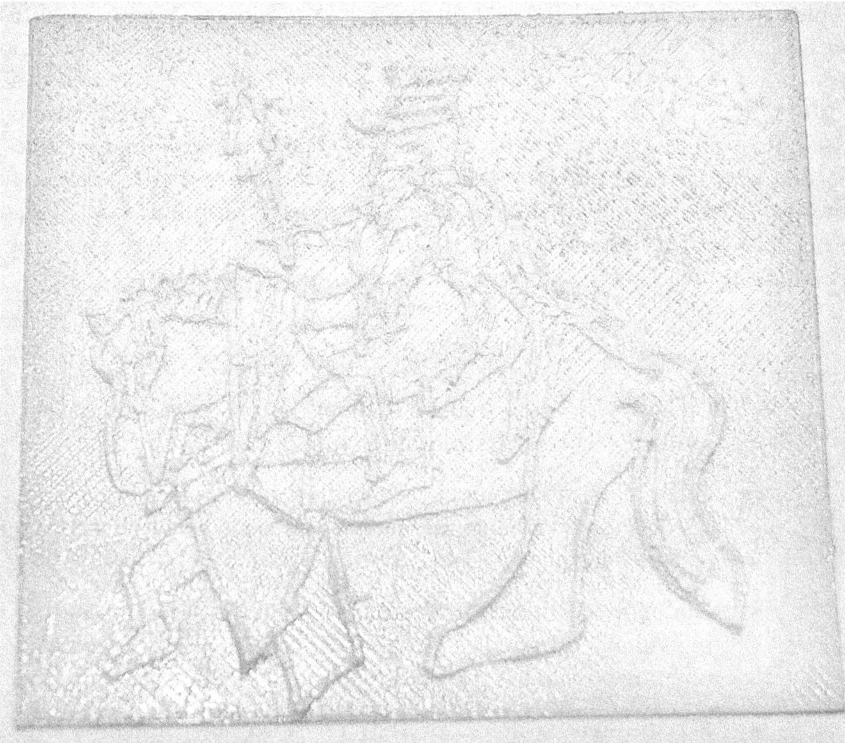

Figure 3.19. Close-up of the relief 3D print of the original "Knight" drawing. This was designed to work like a medieval brass rubbing, whereby if paper is placed over the printed tile, and a crayon applied, an image of the knight will appear on the blank paper.

Conclusion

An ambition of the "In the Making" project had been to co-construct documentary films of our participants as makers, as an explicit attempt to re-situate disabled people as active participants in the world, able to effect change in their immediate environments. However, our co-constructors refused to countenance any such film-making. The researchers were taken aback by the vehemence of the reaction, which typically included phrases such as "I hate the way I look," and "I don't want others to see me like this." The feelings of shame and lack that our participants had internalized were devastating. Our co-constructors were quite content, however, to share their digitally fabricated avatars with the wider research community. One woman who contributed to our project chose to give herself extravagant angel wings. A man transformed himself into a gender-fluid octopus. Others recast themselves as cartoon characters or superhero avatars. Thus, the ways in which people choose to embody themselves in the imaginative field of 3D design may contribute to the work of redefining notions of "normal" and expanding perceptions of "how a body can be done differently" (Bennett et al. 2016, 1754). Thus, the transformative and performative aspects of 3D printing seem to open routes to a re-situating of disabled people in cultural narratives, loaded with the potential for a performance of self which turns outward, to engage, challenge or destabilize the spectator, prompting what Roger Kneebone (2015) describes as "an open-minded exchange of perspectives" resulting in "'*reciprocal illumination*' for everyone who takes part" (861).

Take-aways

- Creative and imaginative thinking are required to make meaningful use of 3D printing technology
- Cultural narratives about who is "creative" can lead marginalized and disadvantaged people to consider themselves excluded from creative activity
- Our project found that simple poetic routines enabled individual and group activity which generated rich material, opening possibilities for wearable text
- 3D printed avatars proved an effective strategy for participants to get around the negative self-perceptions which cultural constructions of disabled people can impose
- Brief, wearable texts proved popular and successful 3D prints with our participants. These texts might be understood as disruptive of established cultural narratives, offering insights into the lived experiences of disabled people who have traditionally been excluded from auto/biographical practices
- Our project encountered difficulties in bringing creative and technical facilitators into the same space. We recommend that more time and resource need to be devoted to developing skillsets and helping professionals communicate effectively with each other.

Chapter 4

Analysis of outputs

This chapter presents detailed case-studies, representing outputs which speak to the three main research strands which underpinned the "In the Making" project. As outlined in Chapter 1, these are:

1. **Entrepreneurial making**: Can "making" become a counter-cultural space in the experience of disability? Might disabled people bring about a cultural shift by casting themselves as innovators, makers and entrepreneurs, creating wealth rather than being seen as a drain on resources?
2. **Political making**: Can critical making be used in campaigning for disability rights? Can it contribute to greater cultural visibility and even policy change? We used DiSalvo's definition of political engagement: "we are doing politics through design when we work together to elucidate and give form to the desires and commitments of a community of practice" (2014, 103-104). This strand linked making to political awareness/activity and sought to explore (dis)connection with political processes.
3. **Creative making:** Can the processes and products of FabLab practice can be "read" as auto/biographical texts? What insights into self-knowledge, self-fashioning, health and well-being might be generated as a result? How might disabled people assert their right to aesthetic/expressive making, beyond the practical and assistive?

Entrepreneurial Making

The 3D printing workshops opened the possibility of "making" as a counter-cultural space in the experience of disability. Disabled people participating in the project explored ways to bring about a cultural shift by casting themselves as innovators, makers and entrepreneurs, creating wealth rather than being seen as a drain on resources. The "In the Making" project investigated the concept of the "blue ocean" (Kim and Mauborgne, 2005) as a means of creating uncontested market space – in this case around the economic role of disabled people. The "blue ocean" approach creates new value in an organization's staff and those who consume its products/services and intellectual capital, while unlocking new demand and making its competitors irrelevant. In a blue ocean (in contrast with a red ocean) the premium is on value innovation. However, as Gershenfeld (2012) notes, "concern about digital fabrication relates to the theft of intellectual property. If products are transmitted as designs and produced on demand, what is to prevent those designs from being replicated without permission?" (47). Alternative models of entrepreneurship need to be co-investigated and solutions co-constructed. "Instead of trying to restrict access, flourishing software businesses have sprung up that freely share their source codes and are compensated for the services they provide" (Gershenfeld 2012, 48). "In the Making" attempted to co-investigate the possibilities of inclusive digital fabrication as a means of connecting disabled people to the digital and knowledge economies, with interested participants being bridged to their local FabLab or makerspace for specialist long term support.

Some makers, for example, came to the sessions with an idea or a need already firmly in mind. Participants worked with product designers to develop bespoke cup-holders for their wheelchair, as the example in Figure 4.1 illustrates:

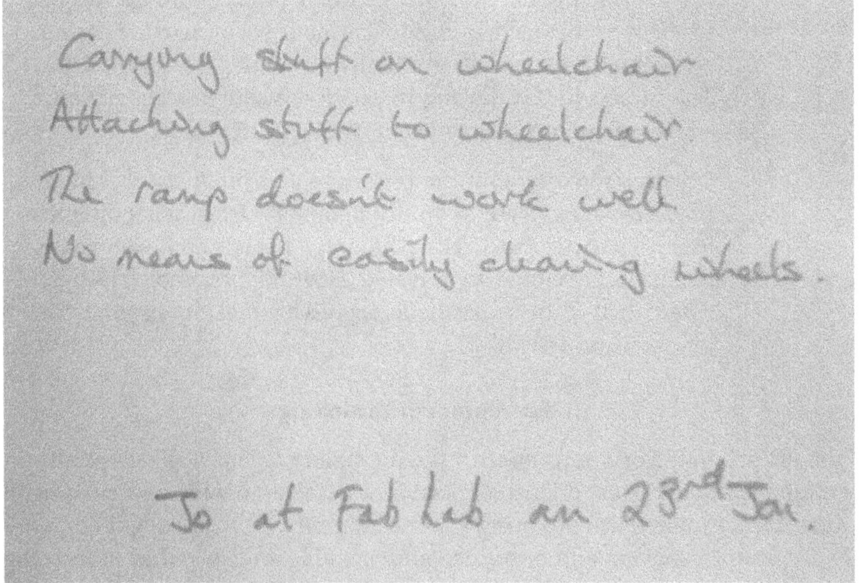

Figure 4.1. This maker came to our workshop with a list of practical needs that might be addressed through digital fabrication. All the needs listed in the illustration revolve around the physical circumstance of using a wheelchair in daily life.

As can be seen in Figure 4.2 in this maker's notebook, which he generously agreed to share with the researchers, people came to the making sessions brimming with ideas and enthusiastic about the possibilities.

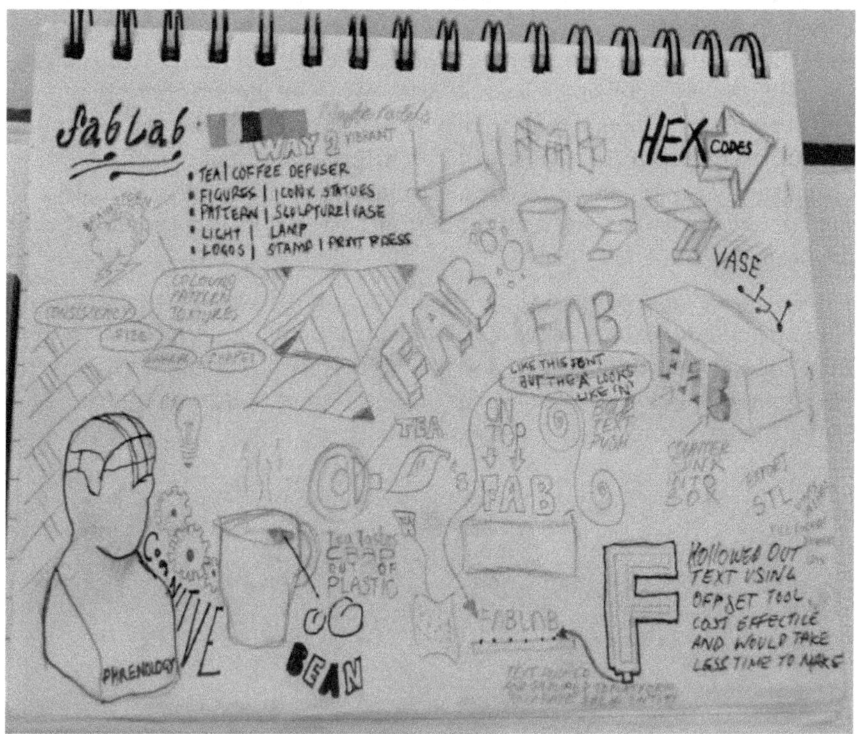

Figure 4.2. This maker had ambitions to study design, but long-term health conditions had prevented him from doing so. Here, we see initial ideas for lamps, vases, a hot drinks diffuser and various logos, stamps and presses for creating visual text.

The technical limitations of our portable, entry-level equipment meant that we had to manage people's expectations carefully. While a diffuser for hot drinks might be a great idea, our printers could only work with plastic that would melt on contact with boiling liquid. The challenge here was to bridge an aspiring designer into connecting with a more sophisticated makerspace facility. While participants had the opportunity to speak with a product designer, and to begin learning the software that they would need to use to bring their prototype to print, the "In the Making" project did not have the resources to mentor people through to market testing. Wherever possible we tried to introduce people to their local FabLab or makerspace, putting them in touch with the Lab manager, or equivalent, in the hope that knowing a name and a friendly face in advance would encourage people to attend the facility.

However, very few participants, to our knowledge, progressed into regular attendance at an established makerspace. Travel difficulties and lack of confidence proved to be too significant for most people to overcome. Reflecting at the end of the project, we were disappointed to find that this stand of the research, which we had expected to be the most visibly present and achievable, remained the least developed. We found in general that routes to entrepreneurship for a novice maker with a good idea were not clearly established, and in fact represent a notable gap in the creative industries in the UK (Symons and Hurley, 2018). Further research and development work are needed in this area.

However, we did have some interesting and positive results with participants who were interested in assistive aids for medical conditions. One artist traveled from London to work with us on developing therapeutic jewelry, which served a prosthetic or supportive function, as well as aesthetic adornment/expression for the wearer. Figure 4.3 shows an early prototype:

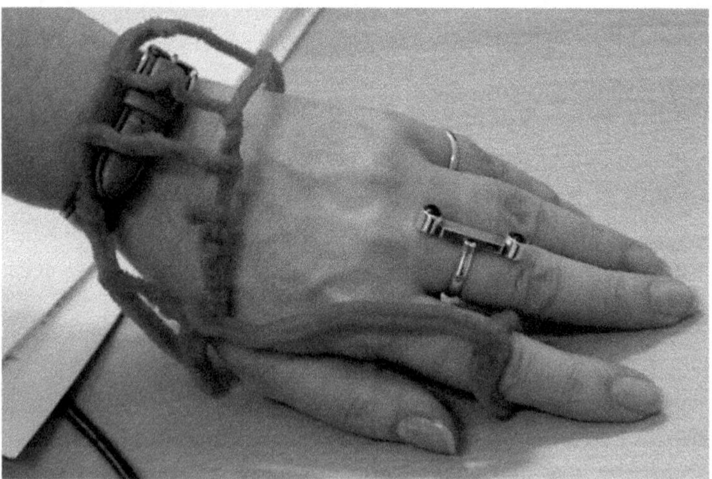

Figure 4.3. A prototype for therapeutic jewelry handmade from pipe-cleaners. Our printers were not able to realize the delicacy and complexity of the design, despite its potential.

We strongly encouraged the maker to continue this work at a makerspace nearer to her home. Ideally, she would need to locate a facility with the capacity to work in metal. Further correspondence with this maker evidenced that she had valued her participation in our makerspace and, as an established artist, felt confident that she could pursue this design in her own locality.

Another maker had more tangible success with a finger splint. She lived with a condition that caused the deterioration of her joints. She had to support the joints in her hands with orthotic splints to avoid the need for corrective surgery. Having been told by her healthcare team that her hands were too small to be fitted with finger splints, and that surgery was inevitable, this maker came to our project determined to prove them wrong. Our participant searched online and found a company in the USA that would make bespoke supports. Their service was costly, and her financial circumstances prevented her from being able to commission a customized splint. However, as Figures 4.4-4.8 show, she downloaded their measuring instructions and progressed a prototype with our product designer.

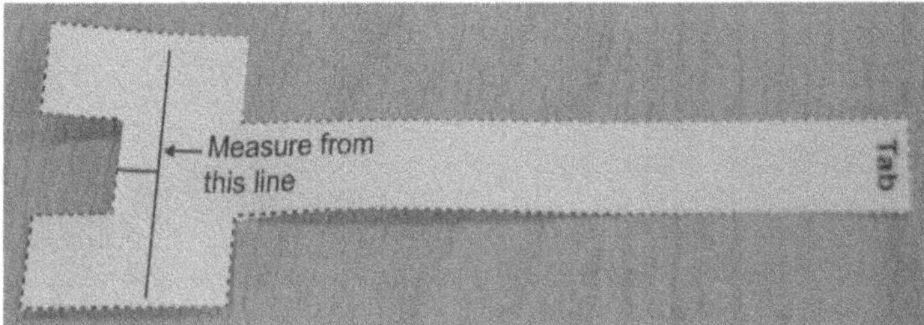

Figure 4.4. This determined maker came to our project with measuring instructions to see if she could make a splint for her finger – something which her healthcare team had told her couldn't be done.

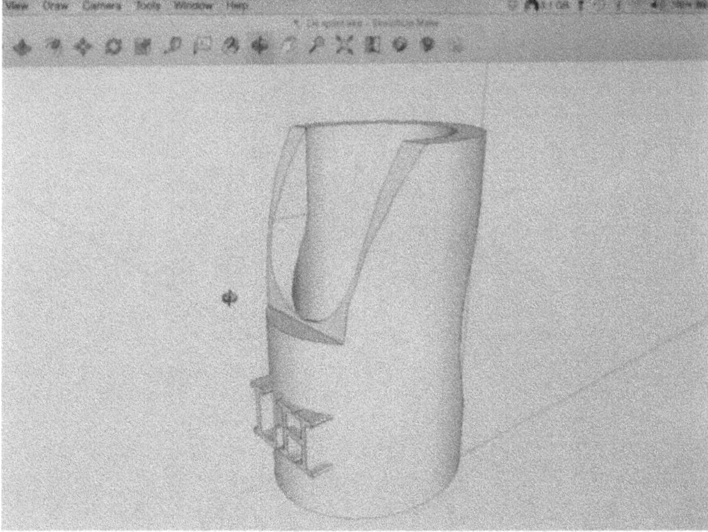

Figure 4.5. Our product designer worked closely with our participant to model a prototype in 3D design software. Here he is using Sketchup – freely available and offering an extensive community of user support.

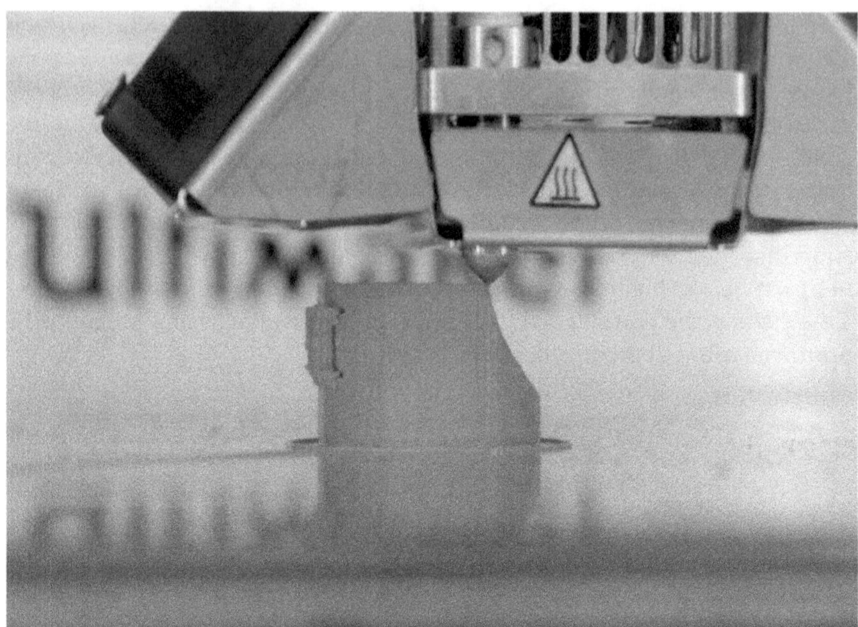

Figure 4.6. The prototype emerging from the print head.

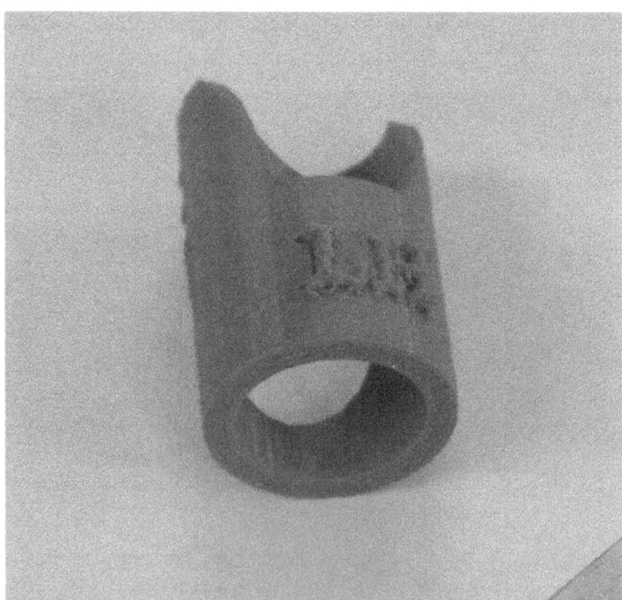

Figure 4.7. The finished prototype. Note that relief initials were added to personalize the splint, and a choice of color was also available (this one is bright pink). This maker had a keen sense of fashion and enjoyed the options to co-ordinate different colored splints with different outfits.

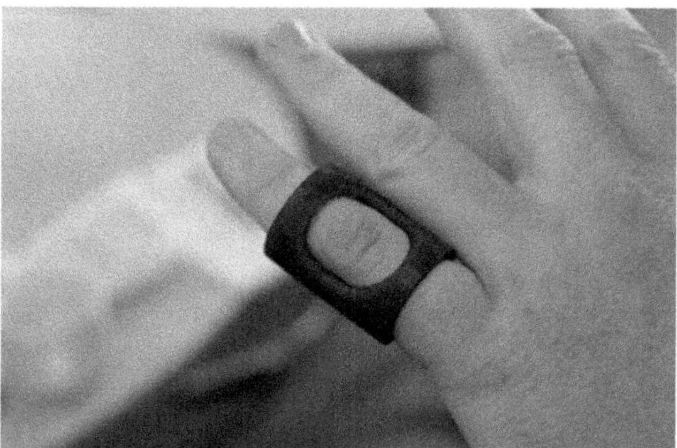

Figure 4.8. In a later version of the prototype, a wearable version is tested. This is not, however, the hand of the maker, who did not want her own hands to be photographed owing to their perceived "deformity" (see earlier discussion of avatars).

The prototype was highly promising, although the plastic was rough and inflexible, meaning that further refinements and an alternative material would be needed for the finished article. Although the final product was not achievable within the confines of our project, the maker reported that she showed the prototype to her therapist, who conceded that the design was sound in principle and could work. Empowered by her making activity, our participant reported in a later interview (2018) that she had gained the confidence to question her healthcare team, and to challenge their conclusion that nothing could be done for her. As is evidenced in the independent project evaluation (see Appendix 1), our participant felt certain that she would not have been empowered to debate with her health professionals, and that she would not have requested them to review their decision had it not been for her engagement with "In the Making".

Perhaps the most practically successful output, in terms of its immediate usefulness to its maker, is the example a young artist whose condition made it very taxing, physically, to hold a paintbrush for long periods. He worked intensively with a product designer, who put in a lot of hours in his own time to develop a working model of a paintbrush holder, as can be seen in Figures 4.9 and 4.10:

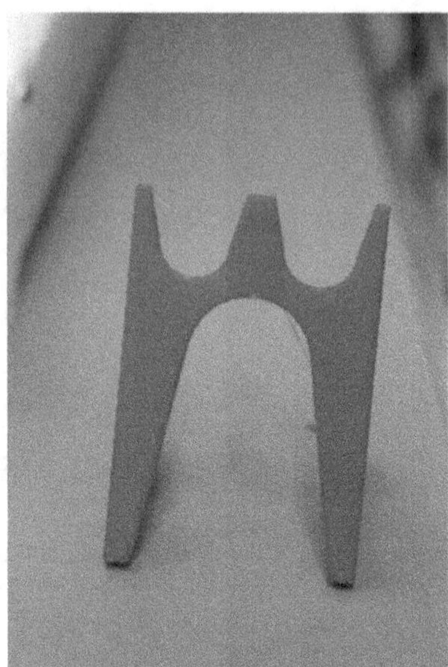

Figure 4.9. Close up of the artist's brush-holder.

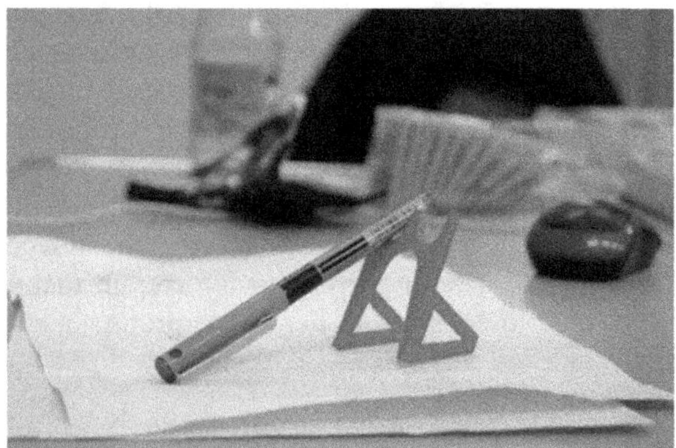

Figure 4.10. The artist's brush-holder, seen demonstrating its principle by supporting a pen.

This maker was pleased with his design, which he was able to begin using immediately as a practical aid in his artistic practice. Project staff encouraged him to develop his concept, and to explore the commercial potential, theorizing that what was useful to one artist could be useful to others. However, entrepreneurship proved incompatible with this maker's identification as a disabled person. Despite being an abundantly talented visual artist (the young man was persuaded to show photographs of his work on his phone), he expressed anxieties over commercializing his work, and stated that he had recently completed a commission without billing the recipient, because he didn't feel that his work was "worth" anything. Despite strong encouragement from our artist facilitators and disability rights workers, he could not be persuaded to see his work as valuable. This may be another example of the internalized self-limiting narratives that were identified earlier. However, it could be that he did not have the energy to pursue the idea, or that he wished to continue working on an altruistic basis. "In the Making" respected his choices – we saw our role as offering people options, not to push them into certain actions.

Conclusion

While entrepreneurial making remained the least developed strand of the project, we did facilitate individual successes around practical assistive aids, as well as showing that digital fabrication can empower people to assert their own needs, offering a route to agency in which those who are usually cast as the passive recipients of care interventions can reframe themselves as makers of their own solutions.

Political making

During the development of the project, we sought to investigate the concept of "critical making", as proposed by Matt Ratto: "a mode of materially productive engagement that is intended to bridge the gap between creative physical and conceptual exploration" (2011, 252). We were interested to explore the politics of disability and identity, as articulated by the things people made. We hoped to use DiSalvo's definition of political engagement: "we are doing politics through design when we work together to elucidate and give form to the desires and commitments of a community of practice" (2014, 103-104). Critical making is based upon participatory, collaborative activities, in which the collective processes of production become tools for co-constructing research, its interpretation and significance: "to engage issues of form and function together with issues of practices and values as they are, or might be, encountered through technological devices[...] giving material substance to [...]desires and commitments—thereby enacting a novel kind of 'doing' of political design as a collaborative and public endeavor of articulation" (DiSalvo 2011, 97). DiSalvo takes care to point out that this approach goes "beyond the user-centered design practices of culling information from potential users, to involving potential users and stakeholders as collaborators in the design process, as themselves designers" (Ibid.).

As our facilitators worked to understand what this might involve in practice, the idea of designing and creating an avatar to represent each participant emerged from collective discussion. As people sketched and glued and looked through magazines, searched the internet and asked each other questions, the collective making space began to develop the idea. What about a fantastical chess set, someone suggested, with each piece being a unique representation of its owner, with a signature move that said something about their character? Great idea but not everyone had played chess, and some were resistant to the rules of a game. What about an avatar to go on a journey? A representation of the self to safely represent the individual on a journey through life. The idea of reality seeming "virtual" is interesting here, and links to the idea that the mainstream world may be puzzling or obtuse for a disabled person because nothing "works" for them. In effect, the physical world disables people who cannot function within ableist parameters.

The world of the imagination, however, may seem more vital, more a territory worth investing in, and one which can be controlled to the imaginer's liking. Using Jessica Symon's facilitation technique (detailed in the previous chapter), the "life journey" avatar was adopted enthusiastically. Then someone asked where we were all going and someone else said, "we have to take an important message". "What would the message be?" asked others. And people busied themselves discussing or writing this urgent message. With constructive questioning from the facilitators, a collective purpose coalesced: the avatars were going to London to give the British Prime Minister a message. Pleasingly, DiSalvo's "collaborative and public endeavor of articulation" (Ibid.) appeared to be emerging. Figure 4.11 depicts an avatar and a message that a young mental health service user designed:

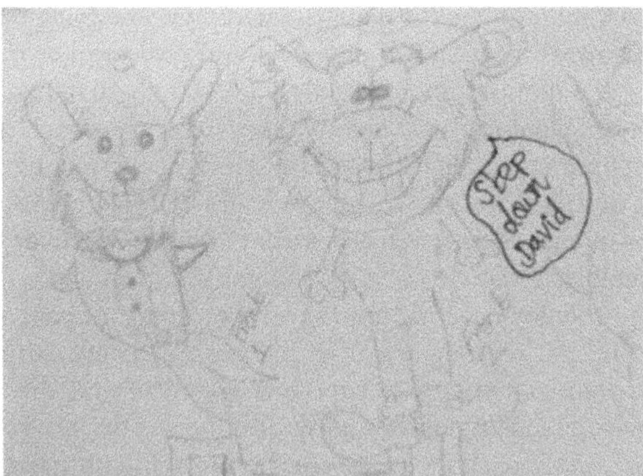

Figure 4.11. "Step down, David" preparatory drawing for a 3D avatar.

This maker designed a cheeky, energetic avatar to journey to London and tell the then British Prime Minister, David Cameron to step down, because she felt he had neglected mental health services in government policy. This is another reference to "austerity Britain" noted earlier.

Playing with things

While the above is an example of a person evolving a strategy to articulate a political critique, some of our participants chose to play with the abstract and fantastical. In theoretical terms, Bill Brown's Thing Theory seems to lend itself to illuminating the concerns and processes of the more abstract or less straightforwardly representative objects that people conceived. Politically, they may be mobilizing non-naturalistic objects' ability to work at the edges of "an amorphous characteristic or frankly irresolvable enigma [...] to hover over the threshold between the nameable and unnameable" (Brown 2001, 4-5).

One participant had encountered disability suddenly and severely in mid-life after suffering a brain injury. He was actively reconstructing himself as an artist and writer, and saw digital fabrication technology, which drew on his pre-injury background as an engineer, as a way of furthering this identity. Lighting on the nub of what appears most interesting in the digital fabrication process, he first produced a piece of wearable text art which featured the word "tactile" very prominently (see Chapter 3 for the methodology of this production). This is illustrated in Figure 4.12:

Figure 4.12. A wearable cuff bearing stars and text in 3D relief: TACTILE ART GENIUS 2015.

Having stated his intentions, the maker then engaged with the visual prompts provided by the facilitators, who had invited participants to create a fantasy creature who could act as their "avatar" in daily life (see Chapter 3). Customizing one of the images, he added the legend "People All Have Skills" to a line drawing of an octopus, giving a strong didactic basis to the art he went on to create. This can be seen in Figure 4.13:

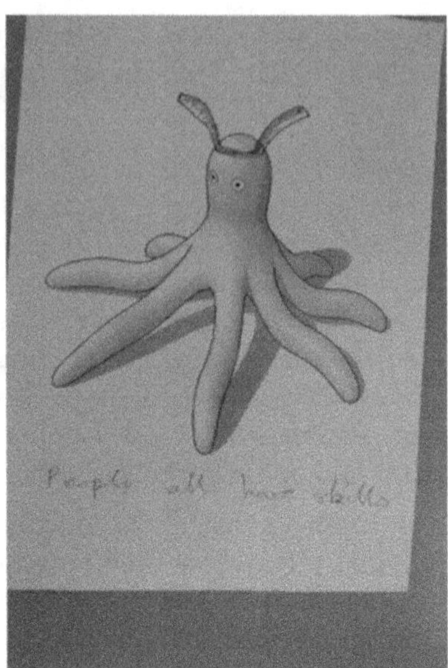

Figure 4.13. A creative prompt image customized by a participant, who gave the octopus ears or antenna, and added the legend "People all have skills."

The political aspect of this making will become more prominent as this account unfolds, and it will be discussed fully in due course. Developing his idea, this maker moved into 3D modelling, riffing on the octopus motif to produce a "creature", shown in Figure 4.14, that defies conventional classification:

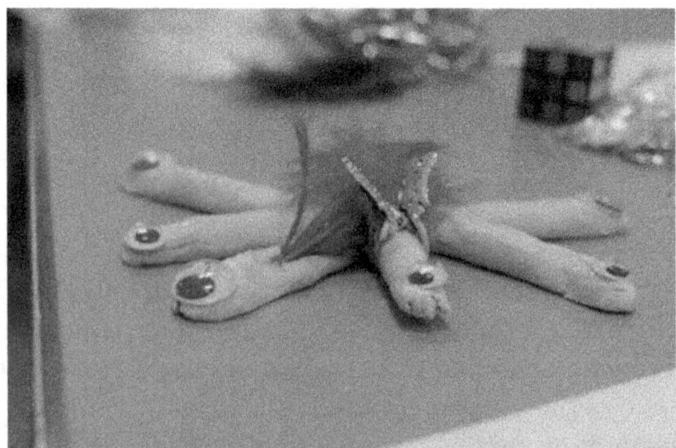

Figure 4.14. The maker was adamant that this prototype was referred to by her full name: "Barbarella, the space octopus."

The prototype sculpture which emerged is distinctive in its refusal of categorization by species or by function. The deliberately feminine touches (the artist was most particular about their arrangement), including the pink feather and the sparkly butterfly jewelry, may signify excess, the carnivalesque, the erotic or seductive elements of the "irresolvable enigma" (Brown 2001, 4-5) of the thing. There are five limbs plus a "stem" instead of the eight found on "real" octopuses, offering something closer to the human hand than tentacles. The eye at the end of each finger/limb emphasizes vision, seeing 360 degrees, looking up, being able to see further, to see into and around, to enquire more deeply into visible reality. This seems to me a knowing exploration of "what is excessive in objects, as what exceeds their mere utilization as objects – their force as a sensuous presence or as a metaphysical presence, the magic by which objects become values, fetishes, idols, and totems" (Brown 2001, 5).

The maker then began to develop his prototype for printing. He intended to create the head and torso of a woman and fuse it with the "legs" of an octopus to create a fantastical chimera. The maker's design was technically demanding, and we were unable to bring it to print within the confines of the project. 3D printers struggle with gravity, and sometimes require support struts to be built into the design, to prevent slender or protruding structures from collapsing before the plastic hardens. However, the thing had been imagined, and the imagining shared via speech and drawing. This maker's idea speaks to sensuality, eroticism, otherness, a refusal of purpose or categorization, lying "beyond the grid of intelligibility" (Ibid.) perhaps as a deliberate refusal to conform to the conventions of a world which no longer works for him. It is not difficult to read into this surreal creation a yearning, perhaps for contact with feminine glamour and the ability to travel at will, which may no longer be accessible for someone living with such a serious injury. But perhaps, as "the Thing is and it isn't" (Ibid.) we may also see it as a means to "both mark and manage uncertainty" (Ibid.) about a future profoundly affected by injury, but also, and positively, to see this creation as a constructive and knowing act of resistance.

One may, perhaps, "read" the "octopus thing" as the statement of an artist whose process is "transforming the bricolage of the dreamwork into the practice of everyday life," and, as such, may denote this maker registering his refusal "to occupy the world as it was" (Brown 2001, 11). Or perhaps, in Heidegger's terms, we might understand this prototype thing and its attendant imaginative existence, spreading pink feathers among the stars, as an acknowledgement that "nothing in the world is adequately expressed by its visible incarnations, since hammers, stars and monkeys will always exceed what we can see or say about them. We can never swallow their reality whole, never us them up through our attempts to formalize them" (Harman 2010, 21).

Bill Brown, in his article "Thing Theory" (2001), offers useful observations which serve as starting points for unpacking the processes described above. What we are doing, when we engage in 3D printing, is making things. Phrases involving "thing" or "things" arose naturally out of people talking about their projects and what they were trying to do. "I'm making something to help with..." or "I'm designing a thing, I'm not sure what it is" were heard frequently in the making space. Often people were designing things whose functions, identities, purposes were emergent, unformed. Some participants played deliberately with fantastical and not obviously useful/intelligible objects. Others were prototyping shapes for situations unique to their own bodies and ways of living – things that did not hitherto exist and belonged to no pre-existing category of object. When Brown writes of "the suddenness with which things seem to assert their presence and power," (2001, 3) he could be describing the presence and power of the newly-materialized 3D print and its effect on the maker.

This observation may apply to any digital fabrication laboratory, where someone succeeds in producing their first 3D print. If, however, we intersect Brown's ideas on things with the lived experience of disability, more specific insights become available: "We begin to confront the thingness of objects when they stop working for us" (2001, 4). Many of the disabled people participating in the workshops described how the everyday world rarely "works" for them. They are forced to confront "things" all the time because even the basic tasks that many of us take for granted become problematic.

Heidegger's tool analysis becomes relevant here. Graham Harman summarizes Heidegger's observation that "our most frequent mode of dealing with things consists not in having them in consciousness, but in taking them for granted as items of everyday use" (2010, 18). Heidegger categorizes things as being either "present at hand", if we are conscious of them because they do not function as expected, or, alternatively, things which are "ready to hand" and used without our being conscious of them because the thing "remains concealed from view in so far as it functions effectively" (Ibid.). Things that do not work "become obtrusive once they no longer function effectively" (Harman 2010, 19). Of course, things can move between one state and another, depending upon their context. But if we consider the world from the perspective of a wheelchair user, for example, almost everything in that world must be "present at hand", and obtrusive in its "brokenness". A simple trip to the shops will most likely involve awkward encounters with street furniture that doesn't "work": steps, curbsides, uneven ground, doors, fire escapes become obstacles to be negotiated. So perhaps from the lived experience of a disabled person, the world can seem overrun with things which don't function, which are "present at hand", while objects which work for them (ready to hand) are rare and difficult to locate. Possibly this emphasis on physical presence accounts in some ways for disabled people's apparent affinity with digital fabrication – the potential to "make something present" on their own terms, rather than dealing with presences continually imposed on them by the ableist world. For some of our participants, the nameless "thingamy" that they design and print to fulfil a function not currently offered by mainstream objects is almost a reversal of the majority experience.

Thus, the "thing" functions straightforwardly, while the mass-produced and commonly understood "intelligible object" does not. Keys are a prevalent example (see the fieldnotes in Chapter 3). Most people see a key and understand its function immediately. For some people with particular physical conditions, however, the key only functions when it is fused with a piece of plastic molded precisely to its owner's grip – something which looks odd and amorphous to the mainstream world. However, the strangely-shaped "thing" makes perfect sense as a lever allowing the key's owner to turn it in the lock, leading back to the ideas of freedom and physical positioning that our collective poem generated (see Chapter 3).

Brown develops this ideological dimension of "things" when he draws on Adorno's thinking, summarizing the point as: "accepting the otherness of things is the condition for accepting otherness as such" (2001, 12). Given that many people who identify themselves as disabled might relate to the experience of otherness, or being "othered" by mainstream society, it follows that participants choosing to play on the margins of intelligibility may be seeking to "recast" things "in the effort to achieve some confrontation with, and transformation of, society" (Ibid.). As Susan Wendell asserts, "There is a cultural gulf between the disabled and the non-disabled; to become disabled is to enter a different world." (1996, 65). Perhaps some sense of that different world, where everyday objects do not work, is what our participants seek to offer those who engage with their intriguing productions.

The postmodern prosthesis

Moving from the consideration of enigmatic objects to an analysis of the text-based cuffs, plaques and brooches that other participants produced (see full account in Chapter 3), we find further political potential. It became helpful to think of our FabLab as a post-anthropocentric makerspace in which hierarchies were overturned, and where machines, animals, expert facilitators and novice makers collaborated to evolve making practices which did not privilege the "perfect reproduction" valued by conventional approaches to digital fabrication. Such a post-anthropocentric maker space provides a link to politically-engaged practice: "the process of making transforms from a way to produce things to a way to inquire about relationships among things, spaces, people and material" (Devendorf et al. 2016, 178). This attention to roles, situations and identities is prompted by digital fabrication technologies engaging space and time, matter and thought. The exploration of such interactions resonates not only with post-humanist criticism, but also with disability studies scholarship. Our project found that digital fabrication is productive for interrogating and recasting experiences of disability because it creates affects of wonder.

Tanya Titchkosky proposes that the affect of wonder prompts those engaged with it to "pay attention to the politics we make use of to respond to the place of disability in our society" (2011, 129). Through identifying and deploying the wonder inherent in digital fabrication, we saw an opportunity to explore how disabled people might situate themselves as makers of their own solutions. We theorized that wonder in the context of 3D printing was located in the technology's ability to materialize the imagination. Titchkosky's articulation of wonder's political aspects helped to develop our thesis. The embodiment of thought made possible by 3D printers might offer a powerful energy in support of what she calls "a reflexive politics of embodied life" (Titchkosky 2011, 132).

Furthermore, the decorative, self-authored wearable texts that our participants generated may resonate with Julia Watson's framing of the post-human prosthetic in auto/biographical production. Traditionally, prosthesis has been understood as "an artificial device that replaces a missing or impaired part of the body" (Bennett et al. 2016, 1746), and usually this has been the understanding with which makers have collaborated with disabled people to provide bespoke medical aids (see the e-NABLE network, discussed in Chapter 2). Watson, however, reclaims prosthesis from its association with lack, and posits it as "a dialectical method of self-engagement, and ultimately a way to reorganize the self-world relationship" (2012, 23). Watson's study focuses on the visual diary-keeping of performance artist Bobby Baker, who documented her experiences of mental illness through an extensive series of dated, often abstract or surreal, self-portraits. The wearable texts produced by our collaborators lend themselves to similar interpretive strategies as they reimagine and challenge the logic of the prosthetic.

One woman with arthritic hands chose the word "overcome." Determined to materialize her sentiment, the participant made the word herself, weaving pipe-cleaners with her own hands, which caused her pain and difficulty but also tremendous satisfaction when she had finished. In engaging with this process, our collaborator fulfills the ethos of the post-anthropocentric maker space where manual interactions with materials ravel the maker in non-human agencies (Devendorf et al. 2016, 175). The progress from writing to materializing can be seen in Figure 4.15:

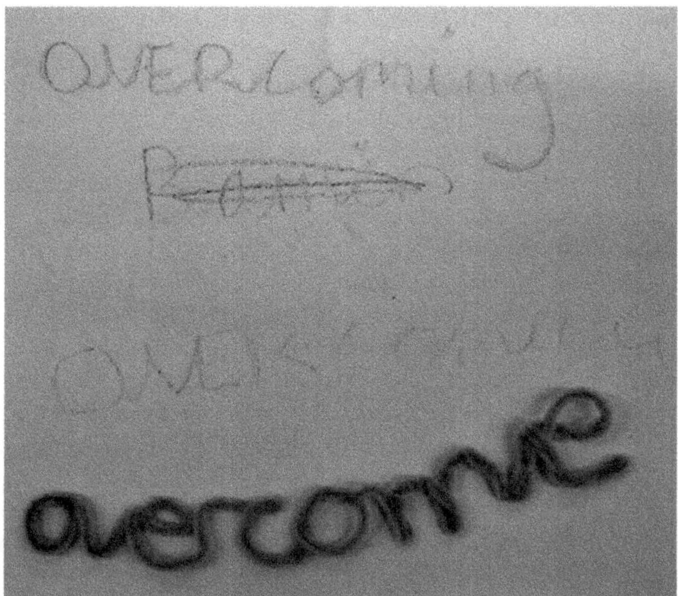

Figure 4.15. The initial written material and the physically-generated text, shaped from pipe-cleaners.

The physical text, embodying the woman's pain and difficulty, was imported via a 3D scanner and sent to the printer, which was able to reproduce this complex, organic lettering as a plaque or pendant in different colors to match its creator's aesthetic preferences. Figure 4.16 shows the printed text emerging:

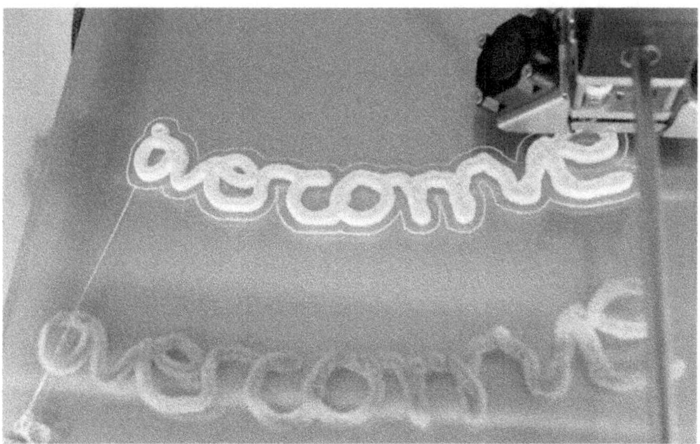

Figure 4.16. The pipe-cleaner lettering emerges from the 3D printer. Note the addition – visible on the left-hand side – of mounting holes to allow the text to hang from a thread or chain.

While the exhortation to "overcome" is inspiring, its meaning deserves a second look. The product of this making may be read initially in the context of the "supercrip" narratives delineated by Couser (2001), stating the wearer's determination to surmount her disabling circumstances. This maker was visibly othered by arthritis. She came to the making sessions in a large electric wheelchair and evidently experienced a constant struggle with pain. She traveled long distances to collaborate with our project, "overcoming" considerable barriers to do so. However, further consideration suggests the word "overcome" as a double-edged, self-reflexive invitation. The non-disabled viewer, encountering this woman wearing a piece of self-made 3D text, is prompted to wonder, to examine and perhaps overcome her own preconceptions about disability. When Watson describes Baker's diary method as a strategy that "shifts the prosthetic from a reactive to a reflexive practice" (2012, 33), she might be talking about our collaborator's activities. Digital fabrication, particularly for those excluded from traditional expressive arts, enables the post-human prosthesis to materialize emotion; to record and share states of being that challenge traditional, humanist notions of self and, ultimately, to place the self "in relation to objects as a process of self-reordering" (Ibid.).

A perhaps more subversive example of this prosthetic potential may be seen in the making activities of a young man with intellectual disabilities. A poet-facilitator collaborated one-to-one with this maker to generate a poem about what he enjoyed. He selected "going out weekends" as the text to be materialized. He typed the text into the computer himself, chose red plastic and stipulated screw holes so that the 3D print could work as a plaque, fixed to the wall of his room. The young man's supporter told us something of the context for this making: a favorite activity was collecting badges and signs; living in a group home, personalizing his room with text and images of his own choosing was very important to him as an assertion of identity. He had never, though, had the opportunity to display text of his own making. The on-screen design for this text can be seen in Figure 4.17:

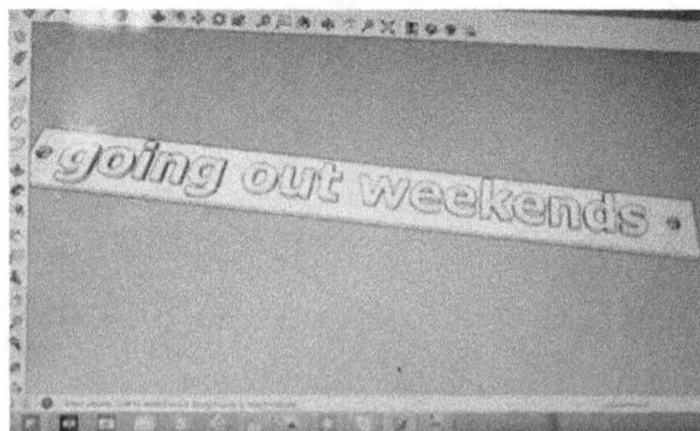

Figure 4.17. The plaque in its digital form. This is scalable, replicable and easily modified. Note the holes for fixing, which the maker helped to measure and position.

The choice expressed in this materialized text may be read in prosthetic terms as an "exercise of agency" (Watson 2012, 36), a statement asserting and affirming the maker's right to social and leisure activities. Cultural narratives about the kind of weekend young people may expect to experience include opportunities to initiate and explore sexual relationships. Such relationships, however, are widely regarded as taboo for people with intellectual disabilities. Michael Gill, in his groundbreaking work *Already Doing It*, points out that individuals "in certain settings such as group homes" are subject to "sexual ableism" (2015, 40). Such attitudes, even among disability rights activists, result in the restriction of sexual liberty for people with intellectual disabilities "primarily because of their impairment label" (Ibid.). In a manner similar to the "overcome" print discussed above, the statement of agency implied in the assertion "going out weekends" is as much a challenge to the viewer's preconceptions as it is a materialization of the maker's desire. Anyone drawing attention to this potential reading of our collaborator's text (as I am now doing) risks implicating themselves in perpetuating sexual ableism, highlighting "the naivete of the individual doing the uncovering" (Gill 2015, 193). The well-intentioned observer, in speaking out on behalf of a perceived "victim" of sexual ableism, becomes aware of her appropriation of another's experience and the double-bind that has made her complicit in reproducing prejudice even as she seeks to address it. The normatively able reader of this print is destabilized in ways which prompt a careful recalibration of attitudes and assumptions, however well-intentioned.

The reflexive and radical potential of the post-human prosthesis, and its relationship to desire, leads us back to the affect of wonder. Not only has this maker mobilized Introna's sense of allure, which "opens the possibility for the radically other to provoke" (2014, 56), but the viewer's sense of self has been "disrupted and unravelled by it" (Introna 2014, 54) and perhaps recruited to "the effort to achieve some confrontation with, and transformation of, society" (Brown 2001, 12). In terms of realizing a politics of wonder, this maker's statement of agency has opened an opportunity to "examine what it means to propose that disability represents personal tragedy, medical substance, and/or restrictions of individual activities addressed and remedied by experts" (Titchkosky 2011, 144). Had he not worked through the process of making via poetry, the maker might not have articulated, for himself and others, this personal and political statement. We might relate this co-constructed, tangible assertion of rights and pleasures to Carl DiSalvo's concept of political making, "as a way of giving material substance to [...] desires and commitments" (2014, 97). Furthermore, we encounter a compelling example of poetic knowledge exceeding the limits of rational, intellectual knowledge to political ends, posing "the question of how we make the meaning of people" (Titchkosky 2011, 131). The politics of wonder is engaged via digitally fabricated expressions of agency.

Conclusion

As this analysis has suggested, the possibilities opened by digital fabrication technologies offer political potential for disabled people who wish to articulate their experiences and to assert their agency. The difficulties and tensions involved in delivering our project prompted us to evolve a post-anthropocentric making space, attending to provisional, unexpected, spontaneous and playful interactions between machine, material and maker. The productiveness of this approach affirms that digital fabrication practices can materialize thoughts and place them in a dynamic relationship with the physical world, that these practices can be inclusive and appealing to disabled people, and that "continued care, experimentation, and growth with a set of materials can form the basis of a sustained relationship with materials that many find pleasurable and even therapeutic" (Devendorf et al. 2016, 172). Beyond the pleasurable and therapeutic benefits of engaging in a post-anthropocentric making space, this analysis asserts that the processes and products of digital fabrication can be read as political inscriptions and assertions of agency. The deployment of 3D printed post-human prostheses troubles the hierarchies of human, machine and material, self-reflexively inviting the re-conceptualization of embodied personhood, the disabled self, and the politics of daily life.

Creative expression

One maker, an art teacher who was medically retired following a serious accident, chose to attend every making session offered by our project, seeking to develop longer-term goals related to her established practice as an exhibiting sculptor. This maker was fascinated by organic, flowing shapes, effects which are difficult to achieve when designing in open-source 3D software. Nonetheless, this maker persisted, stating that she felt there was "something to it", even if results were slow and often disappointing. We worried that our participant might never get to the point of printing a design, given the difficulties of her process. During the facilitation exercises, she would usually sit quietly, listening, but sketching her own work. One day, she seemed particularly inspired, and quickly produced the drawing shown in Figure 4.18:

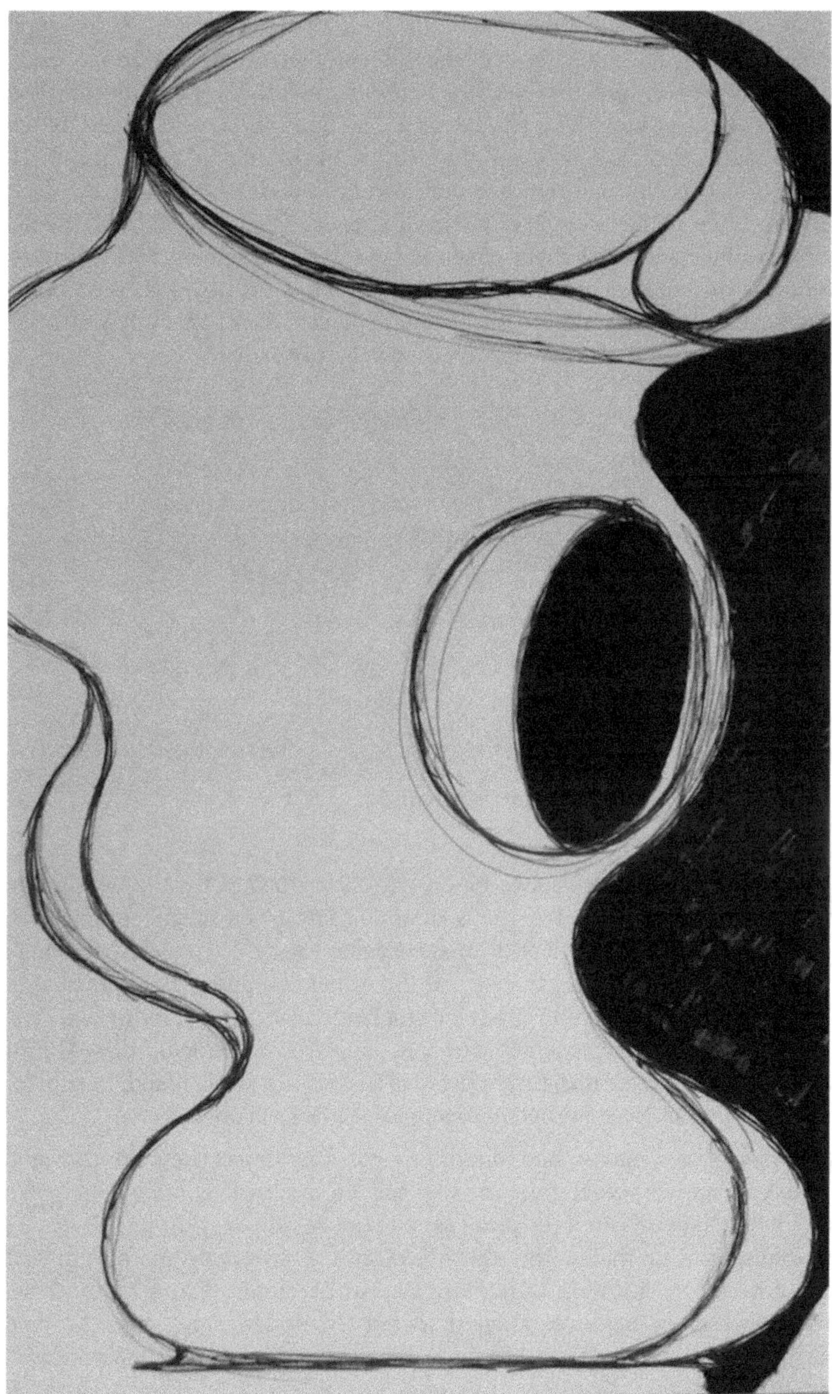

Figure 4.18. A freeform shape designed by a maker with an established sculpting practice.

Our technical experts conferred on the best way to realize this drawing as a three-dimensional shape. Given the difficulty of creating sinuous curves directly in the software, they decided to photograph the line drawing and used the JPEG file as the basis of a 3D design. The lines and shades could be read like topography by the software, to give the beginnings of a 3D object. The design was complex and required our maker to build the 3D shape by tracing organic lines using a mouse. It was important that she did this herself, because the inclusive FabLab casts people as co-designers who learn and interact with the technology, rather than being the recipients of others' technical skills. With renewed purpose, she persisted and after a few technical issues, we printed the shape documented in Figure 4.19:

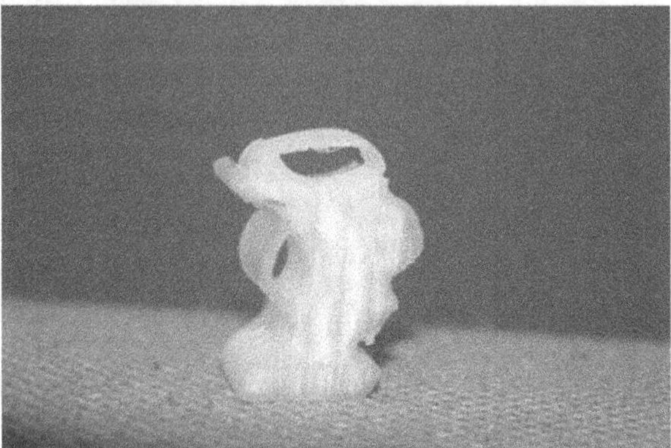

Figure 4.19. Small-scale 3D print of "Freeform".

At first, this print appears to be an odd little trinket. A thing with neither beauty nor function, and perhaps disappointing given all the physical and emotional effort that went into it. Perhaps sensing our concern, this maker contributed to the avatar exercise and the discussion about UK politics, using the topic to give a name and a rationale for her making: the sculpture was called "Freeform Dave". It represented, she said, laughing, the British Prime Minister and the hollowness of the current political situation. It was a bland, transparent grey; wobbly, hollow at the center to represent a lack of conviction.

However, this maker had ambitions for the object beyond the small prototype and a visual pun on the current political context. She talked articulately about her arts practice and what she was trying to explore aesthetically. Our maker saw the object as the prototype for a large-scale sculpture in the tradition of Barbara Hepworth, stating that she could "see" her object on a massive scale, rendered in bronze, now that she could examine and handle the prototype in 360 degrees. Given this maker's careful artistic reflection, we might also read this artwork, in Brown's terms, as representing "the amorphousness out of which objects are materialized" (2001, 5). Or perhaps a representation of "the permanent interplay of light and shadow, one in which reality is never fully manifest to human view" (Harman 2010, 20). Further contexts support and enable these more aesthetically aware readings of the process and product of this making.

Prior to designing this shape, our collaborator had participated in one of the experimental poetry sessions, creating a vivid poem which worked imagistically with black and white, light and shade. For this maker, engaging the techniques of experimental poetry generated a longer-term creative exploration, which crossed media and materialities. This poem is one example, relating clearly to the sinuous black and white sketch shown above in Figure 4.18:

Victory

And climb black blotched branches
Up a rough snow-white trunk
Misunderstanding no more, crispy, dry
I'd like to go climbing a huge, mottled birch tree.

Beginning the poem with "and" suggests that we are glimpsing part of a longer sequence of thought or memory. The feeling of roughness, the details of crispy, dry sounds and textures suggest that this is a memory of embodied experience. The imagery of black and white is also suggestive, particularly as the "black blotched branches" (beautifully alliterated) and the "snow-white trunk" (alluding to fairy-tales and enchanted forests) are followed immediately by the statement: "misunderstanding no more," as though black and white (binary thinking) may be implicated in misunderstanding. Somehow the act of climbing seems to facilitate "misunderstanding no more," as if that physical, embodied experience of moving higher alleviates misunderstandings. Perhaps life is more ambiguous now, and things are rarely as simple as black and white. Perhaps this vivid image is a memory of climbing as a child. There is a sense that if only one could climb (perhaps imaginatively as well as physically) then misunderstanding will be "no more".

Although it is tempting to read this maker's poem in the context of what we know about her status as a disabled person, this poem transcends those distinctions, offering the universal qualities often associated with work considered to have literary merit. Who wouldn't like to climb a huge tree (at least in the space of our imagination)? The relish and joie de vivre in this text evoke idyllic childhood pursuits which, as we get older, we find are less and less possible as physical and cultural constraints combine to deter us. The poem is titled "Victory", but this is arguably not a victory over a physical impairment, it is a triumph of memory and imagination in evoking the freedom of childhood.

Alongside this poem, our collaborator developed monochrome drawings which eventually became the highly abstract print. The choice of pale, almost translucent printing filament may link to the imagery of the snow-white birch tree and its sinuous form, as evoked in the poem. The gaps and absences in the shape may articulate the black blotches or the spaces between branches. But this would be to oversimplify the complexity of her achievement. The print is intriguing and perplexing. It is not identifiable in terms of function. It does not mimetically represent anything in the outside world. And yet it demands our attention. We begin by interrogating its meaning, but then other interpretive strategies become more satisfying. Part of this experience must involve the wonder mentioned earlier: "In the affectedness of allure, I am forced to acknowledge its integrity entirely apart from me – that is, to let it be" (Introna 2014, 52). This idea of allure helps us to understand how the print might suggest an artist "introducing a destabilising subject position which cuts against the dominant ethos" (Deepwell 1998, 107), perhaps even "othering" the viewer in the way that disabled people are usually "othered" by society. We are, to use Introna's terms, "disrupted and unravelled by it" (2014, 54).

Such a reading would support Barrett's suggestion that there are "various ways of 'seeing' auto/biographical texts" which mitigate the tensions between individual subjectivity and its potential to disguise underpinning disabling social structures (2014, 1572). If we accept (at least provisionally) the notion that this maker's print is an auto/biographical text, we might then choose to see the piece as less about her individual circumstances as a disabled person and more about the metaphysical puzzle of "the permanent interplay of light and shadow, one in which reality is never fully manifest to human view" (Harman 2010, 20). Extending the sculptural reading, Barbara Hepworth's writing on her own practice offers further refinements to a strategy for approaching this 3D print: "I became the object. I was the figure in the landscape and every sculpture contained to a greater or lesser degree the ever-changing forms and contours embodying my own response to a given position within the landscape" (qtd. in Deepwell 1998, 107). Similarly, if we trace the development of this maker's sculpture back to the initial poem, we can see the concern with landscape, in this case, the memory landscape containing a large birch tree, and we can situate the sculpture as articulating an imagined impulse or recalled experience of being in a dynamic, embodied relationship with that tree. The material print offers the viewer the chance to share in the embodied experience of memory by holding and touching the maker's memory as "embodied thought." As Introna reminds us, "to touch is to remember" (2014, 55).

What the reader/viewer touches or remembers here is not only an act of embodied auto/biography by a disabled person, but also a complex aesthetic object with its own mysterious reality. Through the shared medium of touch, this materialization of memory and experience is immediately, physically accessible to me, the recipient of the object, although I am not equipped to decode it using my usual analytical strategies. At first, I am in thrall to my human intolerance "for exposure to the seemingly 'useless'" (Introna 2014, 57) and, in my crossness, I realize with pleasure that what this "fleshly encounter" is doing to me "opens the possibility for the radically other to provoke – for the subject to become disturbed, to become its hostage; and as such to become obligated and responsible" (Introna 2014, 56). This obligation unsettles me. I am given the responsibility of responding before I have chosen to accept it. I have been recruited to "the effort to achieve some confrontation with, and transformation of, society" (Brown 2001, 12). The radical auto/biographical potential of digital fabrication is now, I hope, beginning to emerge.

Conclusion

"Many lives [...] go unrepresented, uninscribed because of disability" (Couser 2001, 88). Our project wanted to test the notion that digital fabrication could do auto/biographical work. If so, could it offer ways into inclusive auto/biographical practices that circumvent the traditional prerequisites of literary production (Couser 2001, 79)? In so doing, could it offer ways of "challenging the cultural construction of experiences of impairment as unendingly tragic and/or alien" (Barrett 2014, 1575)? While there is much more research and critical analysis to be done, what I hope to have suggested in this discussion of aesthetic potential is that digital fabrication may offer a way to take advantage of the fact that "subjectivity is not entirely a linguistic construct" (Ibid.) and that it is possible to evoke "a glimpse of a life being lived and communicated [...] beyond or without the resources of what we usually recognize as language or auto/biography" (Ibid.). I seek to open the possibility that digital fabrication and FabLab culture may offer new modes for inclusive auto/biographical practices. In opening these practices, we might begin to identify means to change the story, to destabilize dominant representations of disability through what people choose to make and the stories that those things carry. Digitally fabricated objects might become "delegates that can speak on our behalf, when we are not there to speak" (Introna 2014, 44). And indeed, when we are not able to speak in conventional terms or choose not to speak in marginalizing or disabling language. Or, as Brady puts it: "meaning is unlimited and everybody has some" (2004, 636).

Take-aways

- 3D printing offers new ways into entrepreneurial practice, and may be particularly attractive to disabled people, but new business models are needed to tackle questions around copyright and intellectual property.

- People came to our project brimming with ideas, but they needed longer term, specialist support to bring their products to market.
- Routes to entrepreneurship in the UK digital economy are not clearly established and more work is needed to begin to bridge this gap, particularly if people traditionally excluded from these industries are to contribute.
- People engaging with our project did make promising prototypes for personalised assistive aids. The greatest value in these outputs was perhaps the confidence and sense of agency that these makers developed, leading them to manage their own health issues more proactively.
- The practice of critical making brought people together to collectively address and articulate issues in their lives via shared making practices. Using avatars to speak out and challenge policy makers seemed to be particularly effective with our participants.
- The aesthetic freedom offered by 3D printing encouraged some of our participants to make fantastical or surreal objects, which they engaged to assert the validity of their own experiences and perceptions.
- The possibilities opened by digital fabrication technologies offer political potential for disabled people who wish to articulate their experiences and to assert their agency. This making may include a challenge to the viewer to understand the circumstances of the maker, leading to a greater understanding of those "othered" by mainstream society.
- Digital fabrication and FabLab culture may offer new modes for inclusive auto/biographical practices. In opening these practices, we might begin to identify means to change the story, to destabilize dominant representations of disability through what people choose to make and the stories that those things carry.

Chapter 5

Findings and ways forward

The "In the Making" project explored digital fabrication technologies and their potential to empower disabled people. Interdisciplinary and intersectoral collaboration evolved a mobile, inclusive makerspace. Public engagement with the makerspace established a ground-breaking "proof of concept", demonstrating that people with a wide range of abilities can engage directly with digital fabrication technologies to become "makers" in their own right. These developments go beyond the established precedents for making assistive aids. Via the co-construction of innovative making practices, the project opened routes to aesthetic, political and entrepreneurial achievements by disabled makers. In addition to the wellbeing impacts experienced by individual participants (evidenced in Appendix 1), "In the Making" has established inclusive principles, raised awareness with policy makers, and shown that creative methodologies can widen participation in making practices.

Digital fabrication technologies are established means of producing assistive aids for disabled people. This paradigm situates disabled people as the beneficiaries of interventions from technical experts. Very little work has been done on principles and practices that might empower disabled people as makers of their own solutions. "In the Making" teamed specialists in creative process, human computer interaction, digital fabrication and disability to co-create the UK's first inclusive, mobile FabLab. This makerspace hosted workshops and technical tuition for self-selecting members of the public who identified as disabled. During these activities, the researchers co-constructed investigations into aesthetic, political and entrepreneurial making practices in which disabled people interacted directly with the technology to realize their own designs.

In tandem with the lab activities, site visits and interviews at makerspaces across the UK mapped current facilities and usage. This work identified additional roles that these spaces play: as social spaces, in supporting wellbeing, by serving the needs of the communities in which they are located, and by reaching out to excluded groups. A key finding was that the benefits of engaging with makerspaces extend far beyond the act of making itself, supporting individual wellbeing, contributing to civic life outside the makerspace and enriching social capital. These outputs also propose innovative routes to supporting people with a wide range of access needs, deploying creative practices to widen participation in makerspace cultures and mobilizing that participation in the service of disability rights and/or economic empowerment. The ability to materialize hitherto intangible aspects of selfhood opens new possibilities for auto/biographical inscription and interpretation. These opportunities are pertinent for disabled people, who might engage digital fabrication practices as conscious affirmations of agency, challenging hegemonic cultural narratives of lack and deficiency.

To support these insights, the mobile FabLab co-constructed routines and processes that demystified creativity and reframed it as an adaptive productive process. Such procedures were found to be effective in opening routes for people from different socio-economic backgrounds to participate in the creative economy, widening and deepening the British cultural offer. These findings were achieved by combining the social and political insights of Disability Rights UK, a national campaigning organization, with emergent technology, applying expertise in arts practice and digital technology to investigate the possibilities for societal impact. A number of innovative syntheses have result from this co-constructed investigation, including the co-construction of opportunities for collaborative making with novice FabLab users (disabled and non-disabled) who experienced improved levels of satisfaction and self-esteem in creating and exhibiting work, generating positive narratives of disability which will help to change perceptions. We have co-constructed documentary, reflective and evaluative practices to elicit rich, complex data on the lived experience of disability. Arts practice was demonstrably the key interface between technological developments and social change, establishing a route to impact by generating "human" evidence that policy-makers can use to inform their decisions. This is a transferable methodology.

How the project unfolded

"In the Making" began by assembling a diverse coalition of co-creators. These exchanges brought knowledge exchange between the manufacturing industry, digital fabrication equipment developers/suppliers, local and national charities, the Creative Writing department at Salford University and the Duncan of Jordanstone College of Art and Design at the University of Dundee. Key allies in FabLabs UK, the BBC and local government enabled a 2-day public launch event at the BBC premises, MediaCityUK. Interest from Shaw Trust Ltd. and Ultimaker GB Ltd. resulted in £2500 corporate sponsorship which provided an access fund to pay travel, subsistence, caring and BSL interpretation costs for anyone in need of this extra support, thus widening participation. 60 local people attended, with many expressing enthusiasms for the technology and signing up to participate in further, 2-day training courses. The BBC event led to a special report by Nikki Fox, BBC TV Disability Correspondent. The package featured an expert explanation of the technology as well as interviews with project participants. https://www.bbc.co.uk/news/av/technology-33780101/3d-printing-a-disability-revolution.

Following the launch event, "In the Making" offered in total 96 hours of facilitation to over 100 disabled people, their friends and family members and supporters. Courses were well-attended and some over-subscribed. Many people attended a series of sessions. These co-constructed spaces supported the development of a pedagogical resource by Joe MacLeod-Iredale, a graduate student attached to the project, who produced a thesis entitled "Digital Fabrication for the 99%" (available from this book's website), showing that almost anyone, regardless of ability, can be supported to engage productively with digital fabrication technology. During this time, participants formed friendships, got to know technical experts and developed the confidence and knowledge to move into independent engagement with permanent makerspaces. For example, one participant ran a charity organizing activity for people with autism and attended with a number of her clients, who demonstrated a particular aptitude for the technology. Subsequently, she has begun attending the local makerspace with one of her clients and has taken on an unofficial "greeter" role when she saw the difficulties new attendees could have.

Publicity and positive word-of-mouth communication raised the profile of the project. The researchers were invited to meet Justin Tomlinson MP, then Minister for Disabled People, because he had heard about the project's successful workshops around the Greater Manchester area and expressed interest in its initial findings, particularly with regard to employability and entrepreneurship. The Minister offered his backing for the social development of this technology and asked to be kept informed about the progress of this and subsequent projects: http://blogs.salford.ac.uk/research/2016/03/02/creative-writing-lecturer-invited-to-meet-minister-for-disabled-people/. Following this interest from Government, the research team was invited to submit evidence to the All Party Parliamentary Group on Disability and "In the Making" was cited as an example of good practice in their final report.

The project concluded with a major conference exploring disability and digital fabrication, which took place in the Digital Performance Lab at the University of Salford's MediaCityUK campus in June 2016. Over 50 delegates representing service users, technical experts, policy makers and leading charities came together to discuss the potential of digital fabrication to support economic, physical and mental well-being. The free one-day conference was chaired by Roy O'Shaughnessy, Chief Executive of Shaw Trust and supported by Ultimaker GB Ltd, a leading manufacturer of 3D printers, with demos and design clinics running all day. During the day, service users and policy makers contributed to creative visioning exercises exploring what an accessible FabLab could be, and where our project could go next. Results from the "crowd-sourcing innovation" exercises are informing a follow-on bid. http://www.inthemaking.org.uk/conference/

Project outcomes

"In the Making" has raised the profile of disabled makers and challenged hegemonic narratives about disabled people as the passive recipients of assistive aids. New aesthetic objects have been created as products and as documents of process. Public awareness of and access to digital fabrication technologies has been enhanced, particularly in marginalized and deprived groups. Creative and technical facilitators have learned more about each other's practices, and about the needs and capabilities of disabled people. Awareness of makerspaces and their role in civic society has been raised for local and national policy makers. Beneficiaries include:

- disabled people, who may have experienced positive improvements in wellbeing and self-esteem, and (together with their families, carers and wider communities) now understand more about the potential of digital fabrication/how to access makerspace facilities;
- technical facilitators and manufacturers of digital fabrication equipment, who engaged in knowledge exchange with disabled makers.

Finally, participant testimonials show that disabled people have experienced positive outcomes in terms of confidence, optimism, knowledge, ambition and self-esteem:

> *"Ideas went off in my head and I realized that things are achievable. People will often say 'no' to what you want or need, but it opened my eyes to what can be created."*
>
> *"Today has inspired me to progress my deflated creativeness. Having a non-visual disability can't half get in the way and stop the things we aspire too... but todays atmosphere lifted me, everyone's creative juices were flowing. The relaxed atmosphere and informative tuition was sublime... it helped me interact with people on all levels, sharing ideas and inspirations... I would most certainly recommend this project and would defiantly attend future programs like this. Thank you so much."*

> *"I'm really aware that when I try to describe the up-shot of me taking part it sounds so over-the-top, even to my ears but it really has had a profound effect on my confidence, my thinking and my fear levels. The workshops came along at just the right time and I can't thank you enough for creating this experience. For me it is as much about the people I've met, the sense of optimism and the talk of future possibilities as it has been about discovering the fantastic technology itself. And wherever you take it from here I would really, really love to be involved if I can."*

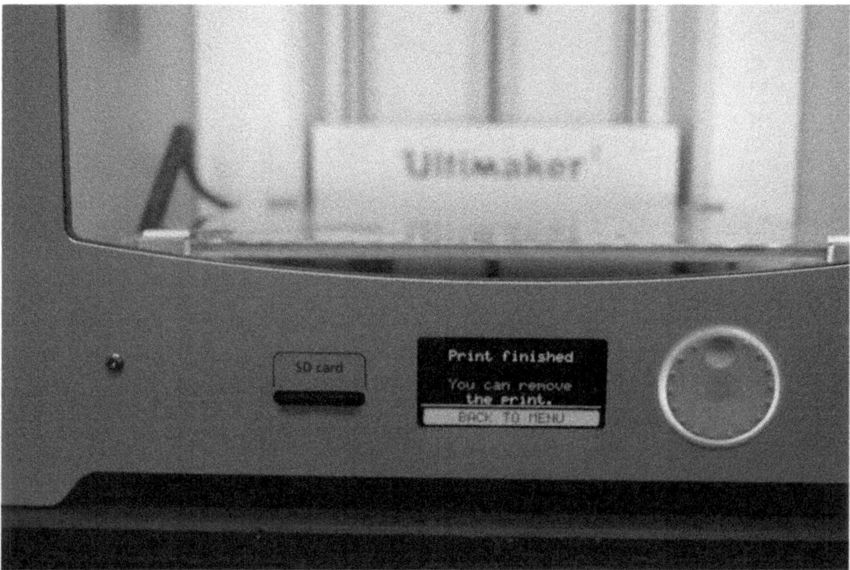

Figure 5.1. Print finished.

Appendix 1

"In the Making" Connected Communities project: an external evaluation

Background

This report provides an external evaluation of the "In the Making" Connected Communities Project, an initiative funded by the Arts and Humanities Research Council (AH/M006026/1). The project's aim was to explore the potential of digital fabrication to empower disabled people as "makers of their own solutions". It offered a series of accessible 3D printing workshops in a range of community venues in Greater Manchester. Six workshops took place between September 2015 and January 2016. The two-day courses were widely advertised, free to attend, and non-selective. The recruitment strategy targeted people who identified themselves as disabled or as having experience with disability (e.g. as a carer), but no one was excluded. Travel, subsistence, and caring costs were met wherever possible. Approximately 100 people engaged with the courses.

What the Course had to Offer

As already noted, the courses ran for two full days at a number of centers in the Greater Manchester region. Each course consisted of:

- Creative facilitation to generate ideas for things to print
- An introduction to 3D design software
- Specialist help from a product designer to use the software
- The opportunity for participants to design and print a prototype.

Methodology

This report provides an external evaluation of the above initiative based on evidence collected from in-depth semi-structured interviews, questionnaires and unsolicited emails from participants. The evaluation took place between May and July 2018. The evaluation was framed in this timescale in order to allow a longitudinal cohort study that could identify any long-term impacts and/or behavioral change as a result of participants' engagement with the project. The timescale (two years) between the original project and this subsequent data collection inevitably means that the perceptions of only a small minority of participants is represented. The complex health needs and diverse communication strategies of many participants pose particular challenges. Despite repeated attempts being made to engage, only a small number of participants were willing or able to participate in the evaluation. Despite the low response rate, it is clear that, for the seven participants represented here, attending the course had been very valuable and worthwhile. The analysis that follows clearly illustrates this.

The Sample

This evaluation revealed that the course was highly successful in attracting a widely diverse group of people. Of the seven respondents, four were female and three were male. They fell into three age ranges, with two aged between 21 and 40, a further three aged between 41 and 60, with the remaining two being over 60. They varied in the level of formal education they had received. One respondent had left school at 16. Another had completed a BTEC course. Two had attained HND, with the remaining three having gained a degree. The participants had come to the course with a range of physical and mental health issues, affecting both their mobility and their capacity to cope socially. Only one respondent had been born with their disability, with the remainder becoming disabled later in life, in one case as the result of an accident. The participants had worked variously in a professional capacity in education and training, advertising, engineering and administration. Only one respondent was currently unemployed. Three of the participants were now retired, two as a result of their disability. Three were actively involved in charity work, either voluntary or paid. Having learned something about the participants themselves, attention now shifts in the next section, to providing an understanding of why they chose to engage with the course.

What attracted participants to the course

Responses fell into two broad categories. Some participants expressed a general interest in learning. Others had a more specific desire to research 3D technology. In a number of cases, participants were exploring the technology's potential to solve problems created by their particular disability; an important outcome being that they gained a sense of ownership of their final products. The course sounded "interesting". It was an opportunity to try "something new". It appealed to a "drive to solve problems". It was "potentially useful" and "life enhancing". Some participants had a strong interest in technology and wanted to learn more. One thought that the course represented "a rare and special opportunity" to do something usually very expensive and complicated. Finally, one participant had a very specific aim in mind - here was an opportunity to learn about a life-changing technology that could take on the "manual work", making it possible to translate artistic ideas.

Impact – A Detailed Analysis

Participant comments are very positive. They represent much of what is to follow, based on a detailed analysis of participants' responses to engaging with this course. From their comments, respondents came away enthusiastic, excited and highly stimulated. For these participants, the course came along at just the right time, providing a reminder of the debilitating impact that disability can have. For one respondent, attending the course has had a profound effect on "confidence, thinking and fear levels". Another respondent was now inspired to rekindle "deflated creativity". The course had enabled the participants to access exciting new technology. But it went further than this. It promoted stimulating social interaction; "creative juices" flowed and "ideas and inspirations" were shared. People came away from the course with a renewed sense of optimism. Some were eager to be involved in any future initiatives. Many of the messages above will emerge again a little later in this report, with evidence presented as four case studies. For now, a more detailed analysis of specific benefits follows. Participants were asked to identify the benefits they had gained from attending the course. They were able to identify a range of positive outcomes, falling into five broad, but overlapping, categories as represented below:

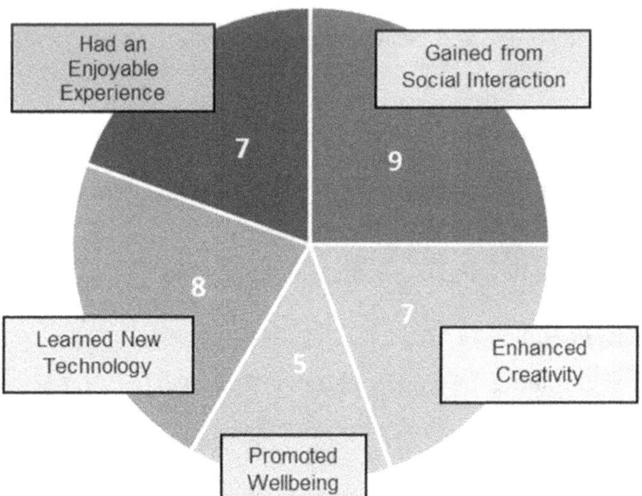

Figure A1.1. Represents graphically the positive outcomes of the provision.

For all 7 respondents, the course had given them the opportunity to engage in a new experience, variously described as "very enjoyable", "stimulating" and "rewarding". Each of the above dimensions is now considered in greater detail:

Learned a New Technology

Respondents gained:

- An awareness of the technology and an understanding of how it works
- Practical skills needed to use the technology
- An insight into the potential of the technology and its uses
- An appreciation of how the technology can be used for their own benefit.

Enhanced Creativity

Gaining confidence in using the technology meant that:

- Participants' horizons had been widened. They could now see how they could make use of the technology creatively
- respondents now had a new tool to overcome their disability and help them realize their creativity.

Gains from Social Interaction

The relaxed atmosphere and positive group interaction meant that participants were:

- stimulated by meeting new people from different backgrounds
- able to exchange ideas and engage in critical discussion, which promoted creativity
- able to develop friendships and networks.

Promoted Wellbeing

As a result of attending the course, participants had:

- Reduced their social anxiety and fear
- renewed their optimism about the future

- gained confidence
- been empowered to improve their personal circumstances.

Impact – Four Case Studies

Case Study 1 – Gaining Access to Cutting Edge Technology

John is a qualified engineer in his late 50's. He has had a varied career. Since 2008 he has been engaged in voluntary work. He is profoundly deaf and has Asperger's syndrome. John retains a passion for engineering and technology but also has a wide range of interests. As a result, he attends numerous courses and workshops. He chose the course because:

> *"it was an extremely rare and special opportunity. CAD, engineering, construction, architecture and 3D printing are very difficult, very complicated and expensive for disabled people to access. It was probably the first accessible 3D course for disabled people in the UK."*

However, the course offered John much more than simply "access". It enabled disabled people to:

> *"... learn, work and communicate. I was also able to meet experts and BSL interpreters... I got to use an Ultimaker, and I learned about the resources available such as the 3D warehouse website."*

All of this clearly stimulated John. Following the course, he has continued to explore 3D technology and its application to art, construction and engineering in a variety of ways:

> *"The 3D Warehouse website has millions of drawings I can access.... I bought two books about AutoCAD and Sketchup.... I have explored the possibility of attending a FabLab in Ellesmere Port."*

Case Study 2 – Promoting New Opportunities, Experiences, Developing Skills

Liz is a female arts graduate in her mid-40's. She has worked variously in administration, customer service, IT support and training. Because of a disabling physical condition, she retired from work 6 years ago. Despite knowing very little about 3D printing beforehand, Liz was attracted to the course because:

> *"I'm always interested in opportunities for disabled people, and as a self-proclaimed 'geek', welcomed the chance to get to grips with a new technology"*

For Liz, the social aspect was a key positive element. She had "enjoyed herself and met interesting people", but the benefits extended beyond this:

> *"The 'hands-on' bit was fantastic; getting to grips with the software and playing around with ideas. I developed my skills and made a bracelet."*

Two years on, Liz remains hugely positive about the course:

> *"New experiences, new skills and new opportunities, Go for it! What's not to like?"*

Case Study 3 – Facilitating Creativity

Helen is in her mid-60's. She is a retired art teacher who retains a passion for sculpture and regularly exhibits her work. She has serious multiple health issues, following a traffic accident.

Helen's attendance at the workshops was, for her, a sustained exploration of how the technology might support her practice as a sculptor:

> *"I get irritated because I can't do everything I want. I can't make things the way I used to. I haven't got the strength or dexterity, so this allows me to realize ideas with the software doing the manual work. I'm hoping to get past this introduction to the software, so I can then explore the possibilities."*

The second part of the comment above indicates that Helen is now seeking to build on the experience she gained on the course to enhance further the quality of the work she produces. The message below is that 3D technology has the potential to facilitate creativity for people currently impaired by their disability:

> *"It makes difficult things really simple. I think this technology is wonderful…the thought of how it could be used. I'm fascinated by the way it allows you to translate your ideas – the interface. It's another tool really. I just want to carry on making things and this is in fact the way forward."*

Case Study 4 – Empowerment: Solving a Practical Problem

Julie uses an electric wheelchair, having been severely disabled since early childhood. She is in her mid-50's. She has had a varied career in office work and administration. She is currently working for a disabled charity. A number of factors influenced Julie's decision to participate in the course. Some were altruistic. She explains:

> *"I do a lot of charity work. I'm very much into inclusion – making sure that people with disabilities get out and socialize and integrate. I like to get involved in lots of things and try to pass on any information I gain."*

For Julie, there were also personal objectives:

> *"My interest in technology is really about how it can enhance my life. I'm very into overcoming problems, so anything that's new and out there, and could help me overcome my disability I'm interested in and I'm going to get involved."*

After attending the first session, Julie found that the course could address a very specific need:

> *"I started to wonder what I could achieve with the technology. I've had long term problems with my hands and trying to get a splint that would fit my fingers and stop them distorting. The medics told me that they couldn't provide me with a splint that would fit – it's caused me a lot of problems. I thought 'I wonder if I could use the 3D workshop to create my own bespoke finger splint?'. So, I tried to design a smaller version that would fit me. When I went to the other sessions I had this goal in mind."*

As a result of the knowledge she gained on the course, Julie now had the confidence to question the medical judgement relating to her case:

> *"After the course, even though my prototype splint hadn't really worked, I thought surely hospitals must be able to produce different sized splints using this technology. I researched it and I found, in fact, there were different sizes. I explained this to the physio. She checked and said 'yes, you're right". So, in the end, I did get the splint."*

Clearly, the course had empowered Julie. As she herself concluded:

> *"If I hadn't done the course I would never have had the knowledge to check this out or the confidence to question the medics."*

Making the Course Better

Participants were asked to reflect on their experience and identify aspects which could be addressed to enhance learning quality. All respondents were very positive about the learning experience that had been offered. However, they did identify a number of issues that they felt should be addressed to enhance its quality. A number of issues emerged, falling into two broad categories, "logistics" and "sensitivity to learner needs".

Logistics

The course lasted only two days and inevitably had limitations.

Respondents felt that in its current form, the course was too short, with the result that:

- instruction was crammed, and they were only able to receive limited personal attention
- they did not have long enough to produce a working prototype
- they encountered bottlenecks caused by the lengthy printing process.

All participants would have welcomed the opportunity to take part in a longer course.

Sensitivity to Learner Needs

Organizers need to be aware of the following:

- sitting for long periods can be painful
- having sessions on consecutive days can be challenging for disabled people
- participants have different levels of technical ability/knowledge

Finally, greater attention should be given to publicizing more widely what FabLabs have to offer. Although several participants were actively engaged in community work and considered themselves "clued-up" about local provision, they had been unaware of the facilities on offer prior to this initiative.

The Way Forward

> *"I would like the chance to develop my skills through work on individual, group and community projects."*

> *"I would have the course going on for longer, more sessions and smaller groups, maybe a max of 5 people, and maybe try and have two levels – one for those who are a bit more tech savvy or have experience in it, and one for those who are less."*
>
> *"My preferred format would be a fixed time per week, so there was a greater incentive to go and the opportunity to build community.*
>
> *"I'd love to do a structured course – 10 sessions would be great. It would be nice to combine that with a drop-in facility after you've completed the course. You might even get that confident that you could teach it to others."*
>
> *"I would definitely be interested in a further course. I'd especially like to get a qualification to assist or teach others."*

For these seven participants, attending this course is just the beginning. There is a strong appetite for further study. All seven respondents would like to attend another course. Six were emphatically positive about this. The five comments sequenced above provide an insight into what the respondents are looking for. Within this sample, four favored a longer structured course (possibly involving up to ten weekly sessions) that would lead to a qualification and "build relationships and community". Two participants required the provision to be sufficiently rigorous that it would qualify them to teach. One participant favored a less structured approach offering "drop-in" sessions. Another favored a hybrid approach combining formal provision with a drop-in facility. Whatever form the course might take, provision should be geographically accessible. Other suggestions emerged. Individual respondents wanted:

- a comprehensive course covering all aspects of the technology and its applications (e.g. in engineering, architecture, design and art)
- differentiation - course provision should consider the differing technical abilities/knowledge of participants
- variety - a mix of individual and group projects
- connection to the real world - off-campus trips to printing centers to see professional projects in action

Notes

Independent report by Nick Astle at Challenge Multimedia and Ian Taylor, Senior Research Fellow at the University of Liverpool, November 2018.

Commissioned by the University of Salford and funded by Shaw Trust and the University of Salford's Impact Fund.

Bibliography

Anderson, Chris. *Makers: The New Industrial Revolution.* London: Crown Business, 2012.

Armson, David. Personal interview. April 29, 2015.

Babineaux, Ryan, and John D Krumboltz. *Fail Fast, Fail Often: How Losing Can Help You Win.* New York: Tarcher, 2013.

Baker, Sarah. "'It's Not About Candy.' Music, Sexiness and Girls' Serious Play in After School Care." *International Journal of Cultural Studies* 7, no.4 (2004): 197-212.

Barrett, Timothy. "De-individualising Auto/biography: A Reconsideration of the Role of Auto/biographical Life Writing within Disability Studies." *Disability and Society* 29, no.10 (2014): 1569–1582.

Barron, Carrie. "Creativity, Happiness and Your Own Two Hands: How Meaningful Hand Use Enhances Well-being." *Psychology Today,* May 3, 2012, https://www.psychologytoday.com/gb/blog/the-creativity-cure/201205/creativity-happiness-and-your-own-two-hands

Barron, Frank. *Creative Person and Creative Process.* Oxford, England: Holt, Rinehart, and Winston, 1969.

BBC. "UN: 'Grave' disability rights violations under UK reforms." *News,* November 7, 2016, https://www.bbc.co.uk/news/uk-37899305

Bennett, Cynthia L., Keting Cen, Katherine M. Steele and Daniela K. Rosner. "An Intimate Laboratory? Prostheses as a Tool for Experimenting with Identity and Normalcy." *Physical Disability and Assistive Technologies* #chi4good, CHI 2016, San Jose, CA, USA. 1745 – 1756, https://dl.acm.org/citation.cfm?doid=2858036

Brady, Ivan. "In Defense of the Sensual: Meaning Construction in Ethnography and Poetics." *Qualitative Inquiry* 10, no.4 (2004): 622–644.

Briant, Emma, Nick Watson, Greg Philo and Inclusion London. "Bad News for Disabled People: How the Newspapers are Reporting Disability". *Strathclyde Centre for Disability Research and Glasgow Media Unit, The University of Glasgow,* November 18, 2011, http://eprints.gla.ac.uk/57499/

Brown, Bill. "Thing Theory." *Critical Inquiry* 28, no.1 (2001): 1-22.

Cabinet Office. 2005."Improving the Life Chances of Disabled People." *Prime Minister's Strategy Unit,* January 2005, http://www.disability.co.uk/sites/default/files/resources/Improving%20Life%20Chances.pdf

Childers, Joseph and Gary Hentzi. *The Columbia Dictionary of Modern Literary and Cultural Criticism.* New York: Columbia University Press. 1995.

Chittenden, Hilary. 2014. "How to Make a Make Space." *Research and Action Centre, Design and Society,* April, 2014, http://www.rsablogs.org.uk/2014/design-society/space/

Connolly, Philip. Personal interview. 12 Jun. 2017.

Couser, G. Thomas. "Conflicting Paradigms: The Rhetorics of Disability Memoir." In *Embodied Rhetorics: Disability in Language and Culture,* edited by James C. Wilson and Cynthia Lewiecki-Wilson, 78–91. Carbondale: Southern Illinois University Press, 2001.

Deepwell, Katy. "Hepworth and her Critics." In *Women Artists and Modernism,* edited by Katy Deepwell, 97–111. Manchester: Manchester University Press, 1998.

Department for Communities and Local Government. "Annual Report and Accounts." *Crown Copyright,* July 1, 2015, https://assets.publishing.service.gov.uk/government/uploads/system/uploads/attachment_data/file/440498/50208_HC_21_DCLG_2014-15_print.pdf

Department for Work and Pensions. "Disability Facts and Figures." January 16, 2014, https://www.gov.uk/government/publications/disability-facts-and-figures/disability-facts-and-figures

Devendorf, Laura, Abigail DeKosnik, Kate Mattingly and Kimiko Ryokai. "Probing the Potential of Post-Anthropocentric 3D Printing." *Printing/Proxies.* DIS 2016, June 4-8, Brisbane, Australia. 170-181, https://dl.acm.org/citation.cfm?doid=2901790.2901879

Dickel, Sascha and Jan-Felix Schrape. "The Logic of Digital Utopianism." *NanoEthics* 11, no.1 (2017): 47-58, DOI: 10.1007/s11569-017-0285-6

DiSalvo, Carl. "Critical Making as Materializing the Politics of Design." *The Information Society: An International Journal* 30, no.2 (2014): 96-105.

Elliot, Andrew J, and Todd M Thrash. "The Intergenerational Transmission of Fear of Failure." *Personality and Social Psychology Bulletin* 30, no.8 (2004): 957-971.

Gallix, Andrew. "Oulipo: Freeing Literature by Tightening its Rules." *The Guardian,* July 12, 2013, https://www.theguardian.com/books/booksblog/2013/jul/12/oulipo-freeing-literature-tightening-rules

Gershenfeld, Neil. *Fab: The Coming Revolution on Your Desktop—From Personal Computers to Personal Fabrication,* New York: Basic Books, 2005.

Gershenfeld, Neil. "How to Make Almost Anything." *Foreign Affairs* 91, no.6 (2012): 42-57.

Gill, Michael. *Already Doing It: Intellectual Disability and Sexual Agency.* Minneapolis: University of Minnesota Press, 2015.

Goldsmith, Ronald E. and Timothy A. Matherly. "Creativity and Self-Esteem: A Multiple Operationalization Validity Study." *Journal of Psychology* 122, no. 1 (1988): 47-57.

Gross, David. "'Mind-Forg'd Manacles': Hegemony and Counter-Hegemony in Blake." *The Eighteenth Century* 27, no. 1 (1986): 3-25, http://www.jstor.org/stable/41467368

Hall, Doug. "Fail fast, fail cheap." *Business Week* 32 (2007): 19-24.

Haraway, Donna J. *Simians, Cyborgs and Women: The Reinvention of Nature.* London: Free Association Books, 1991.

Harman, Graham. 2010. "Technology, Objects and Things in Heidegger." *Cambridge Journal of Economics* 34 (2010): 17-25.

Hielscher, Sabine and Adrian Smith. 2014. "Community-based Digital Fabrication Workshops: A Review of the Research Literature." *Science and Technology Policy Research Unit, University of Sussex,* May 21, 2014, http://dx.doi.org/10.2139/ssrn.2742121

Ingold, Tim and Elizabeth Hallam. *Creativity and cultural improvisation.* Oxford/New York: Berg, 2007.

Introna, Lucas D. "Ethics and Flesh." In *Ruin Memories, Materiality, Aesthetics and the Archaeology of the Recent Past,* edited by Bjørnar Olsen and Þóra Pétursdóttir 41-61. London: Routledge, 2014.

Jackson, Carolyn. "Motives for 'Laddishness' at School: Fear of Failure and Fear of the 'Feminine'." *British Educational Research Journal* 29, no. 4 (2003): 583-598.

Jackson, Norman. *Creativity in Higher Education.* Lancaster: The Higher Education Academy/PALATINE, 2003.

Jameson, Frederic. *The Cultural Turn: Selected Writings on the Postmodern, 1983-1998.* Verso: London and New York, 1998.

Kim, W. Chan and Renée Mauborgne. *Blue Ocean Strategy: How to Create Uncontested Market Space and Make Competition Irrelevant.* Brighton, Massachusetts: Harvard Business Publishing, 2005.

Kneebone, Roger. "When I say ... Reciprocal Illumination." *Medical Education* 49 (2015): 861-862, doi:10.1111/medu.12743

Landay, James A. "Technical Perspective: Design Tools for the Rest of Us," *Communications of the ACM* 52, no. 12 (December 2009): 80, DOI:10.1145/1610252.1610274

Lau, Manfred, Jun Mitani and Takeo Igarashi. "Digital Fabrication." *Computer* 45, no.12 (2012): 76-79.

Leach, James. "Drum and Voice: Aesthetics and Social Process on the Rai Coast of Papua New Guinea." *Journal of the Royal Anthropological Institute* 8, no.4 (2002): 713-735.

MacLeod-Iredale, Joe. "Digital Fabrication for the 99%." Master's Thesis, University of Salford, 2016.

Naray-Davey, Szilvia and Ursula Hurley. "Fail Again, Fail Better: The Case for Formative Assessment in First-Year Undergraduate Creative Practice-Based Modules." *The International Journal of the Arts in Education* 8, no.3 (2014): 1-13.

Nelson, Bryan. "Scientists closer to creating a 'Star Trek'-style replicator." *Mother Nature Network,* 2015, https://www.mnn.com/green-tech/research-innovations/stories/scientists-closer-creating-star-trek-style-replicator. Date accessed: 1 May 2018.

Nemorin, Selena. "The Frustrations of Digital Fabrication: An Auto/Ethnographic Exploration of '3D Making in School'." *International Journal of Technology and Design Education* 27, no.4 (2017): 517–535, https://doi-org.salford.idm.oclc.org/10.1007/s10798-016-9366-z

Phelps, Nicholas A. "The Sub-Creative Economy of the Suburbs in Question." *International Journal of Cultural Studies* 15, no.3 (2012): 259-271.

Ratto, Matt. "Critical Making: Conceptual and Material Studies in Technology and Social Life." *The Information Society* 27, no.4 (2011): 252–60.

Richards, Ruth. "Everyday creativity: Our hidden potential." In *Everyday Creativity and New Views of Human Nature: Psychological, Social, and Spiritual Perspectives,* edited by Ruth Richards 3-22. Washington, DC: American Psychological Association, 2007.

Richards, Ruth. "Everyday Creativity." In *The Cambridge Handbook of Creativity*, edited by James C. Kaufman & Robert J. Sternberg 189-215. Cambridge: Cambridge University Press, 2010, doi:10.1017/CBO9780511763205.013

Silvia, Paul J., Roger E. Beaty, Emily C. Nusbaum, Kari M. Eddington, Holly Levin-Aspenson and Thomas R. Kwapi. "Everyday Creativity in Daily Life: An Experience-Sampling Study of 'Little c' Creativity." *Psychology of Aesthetics, Creativity, and the Arts* 8, no.2 (2014): 183-188.

Smith, Hazel. *The Writing Experiment: Strategies for Innovative Creative Writing*. London: Allen and Unwin, 2005.

Su, Ya-Hui. "Idea creation: the need to develop creativity in lifelong learning practices." *International Journal of Lifelong Education* 28, no.6 (2009): 705-717.

Symons, Jessica. "Untangling Creativity and Art for Policy Purposes: Ethnographic Insights on Manchester International Festival and Manchester Day Parade." *International Journal of Cultural Policy*24, no.2 (2016): 205-219, DOI: 10.1080/10286632.2016.1150268

Symons, Jessica and Ursula Hurley. "Strategies for Connecting Low Income Communities to the Creative Economy Through Play: Two Case Studies in Northern England." *Creative Industries Journal* 11, no.2 (2018): 121-136, DOI: 10.1080/17510694.2018.1453770

Titchkosky, Tanya. *The Question of Access: Disability, Space, Meaning*. Toronto: University of Toronto Press, 2011.

Walter-Herrmann, Julia and Corinne Büching, 'Notes on Fab Labs.' In: Julia Walter-Herrmann and Corinne Büching (eds.), *FabLab: of Machines, Makers and Inventors*. Bielefeld: Transcript Verlag, 2013, 9–26. (10)

Watson, Julia. "Visual Diary as Prosthetic Practice in Bobby Baker's *Diary Drawings*." *Biography* 35, no.1 (Winter 2012): 21-44.

Weingartner, Charles. "MIND FORG'D MANACLES..." *Educational Studies* 8, no.1 (1997): 21-27.

Wendell, Susan. *The Rejected Body: Feminist Philosophical Reflections on Disability*. New York: Routledge, 1996.

Wexler, Alice and John Derby. "Art in Institutions: The Emergence of (Disabled) Outsiders." *Studies in Art Education: A Journal of Issues and Research* 56, no.2 (2015): 127-141.

Wylie, Sara Ann, Kirk Jalbert, Shannon Dosemagen and Matt Ratto. "Institutions for Civic Technoscience: How Critical Making is Transforming Environmental Research." *The Information Society: An International Journal* 30, no.2 (2014): 116-126.

Index

3

5

A

B

C

D

E

R

S

T

U

V

W

X

www.ingramcontent.com/pod-product-compliance
Lightning Source LLC
LaVergne TN
LVHW020634100826
845148LV00012B/2181